TELEVISION AND CHILDREN

The SAGE CommText Series

Series Editor:
EVERETTE E. DENNIS
Gannett Center for Media Studies, Columbia University

Founding Editor: F. GERALD KLINE, *late of the School of Journalism and Mass Communication, University of Minnesota*
Founding Associate Editor: SUSAN H. EVANS, *Annenberg School of Communications, University of Southern California*

The **SAGE CommText** series brings the substance of mass communication scholarship to student audiences by blending syntheses of current research with applied ideas in concise, moderately priced volumes. Designed for use both as supplementary readings and as "modules" with which the teacher can "create" a new text, the **SAGE CommTexts** give students a conceptual map of the field of communication and media research. Some books examine topical areas and issues; others discuss the implications of particular media; still others treat methods and tools used by communication scholars. Written by leading researchers with the student in mind, the **SAGE CommTexts** provide teachers in communication and journalism with solid supplementary materials.

Available in this series:

1. TELEVISION IN AMERICA
   George Comstock
2. COMMUNICATION HISTORY
   John D. Stevens and Hazel Dicken Garcia
3. PRIME-TIME TELEVISION: Content and Control
   Muriel G. Cantor
4. MOVIES AS MASS COMMUNICATION
   Garth Jowett and James M. Linton
5. CONTENT ANALYSIS: An Introduction to Its Methodology
   Klaus Krippendorff
6. INTERPERSONAL COMMUNICATION: The Social Exchange Approach
   Michael E. Roloff
7. THE CARTOON: Communication to the Quick
   Randall P. Harrison
8. ADVERTISING AND SOCIAL CHANGE
   Ronald Berman
9. COMPARATIVE COMMUNICATION RESEARCH
   Alex S. Edelstein
10. MEDIA ANALYSIS TECHNIQUES
    Arthur Asa Berger
11. SHAPING THE FIRST AMENDMENT: The Development of Free Expression
    John D. Stevens
12. THE SOAP OPERA
    Muriel G. Cantor and Suzanne Pingree
13. THE DISSIDENT PRESS: Alternative Journalism in American History
    Lauren Kessler
14. TELEVISION AND CHILDREN: A Special Medium for a Special Audience
    Aimee Dorr

additional titles in preparation

Aimée Dorr

TELEVISION AND CHILDREN

A Special Medium for a Special Audience

Volume 14. The Sage CommText Series

SAGE PUBLICATIONS
The Publishers of Professional Social Science
Beverly Hills London New Delhi

To the Many Students
Who Stimulated My Thinking
and
To Don, Simeon, and J. T.
Who Gave Me Inspiration, Insight, and Time

For information address:

SAGE Publications, Inc.
275 South Beverly Drive
Beverly Hills, California 90212

SAGE Publications India Pvt. Ltd.
M-32 Market
Greater Kailash I
New Delhi 110 048 India

SAGE Publications Ltd
28 Banner Street
London EC1Y 8QE
England

Printed in the United States of America

Library of Congress Cataloging-in-Publication Data

Dorr, Aimée.
Television and children.

(The Sage commtext series ; v. 14)
Bibliography: p.
Includes index.
1. Television and children—United States.
I. Title. II. Series.
HQ784.T4D67 1986 791.45'01'3 85-19675
ISBN 0-8039-2568-9
ISBN 0-8039-2565-4 (pbk.)

FIRST PRINTING

CONTENTS

1

A SPECIAL MEDIUM FOR A SPECIAL AUDIENCE

Television is a ubiquitous medium whose carefully constructed, often realistic content attracts children who—simply because they are children—are neither very skilled at making sense of television content nor very knowledgeable about the real-life world television seems to depict.

In 1955 when the British psychologist Hilde Himmelweit began her pioneering study, *Television and the Child,* she could unequivocally assert that "there were few facts available about children's behaviour and reactions to viewing" (Himmelweit, Oppenheim, & Vince, 1958, p. xiii). Twenty-five years later, one bibliographer compiled nearly 2500 English-language citations about children and television (Murray, 1980). Such phenomenal growth in research and commentary reflects the academic community's belief in the social importance and intellectual challenge of this topic. That conviction continues today.

Although most Americans treat television as just another piece of furniture or a slightly odd member of the family, many parents, teachers, social commentators, and social scientists realize that television provides important experiences for children growing up today. It is a medium whose technical capabilities and circumstances of use set it apart from other media. Children turn to it regularly for entertainment and enlightenment presented in realistic, believable programs and commercials. They come to it as a special audience, with incomplete understanding of the physical and social world in which they live, eager to learn, and somewhat limited in their abilities. Television offers them an enthralling world to try to understand and from which to learn.

Obviously, television is not children's only socialization agent nor is it a medium entirely different from other media. Just as obviously, children are not a monolithic, undifferentiated group nor are they entirely different from adult television viewers. Because of these points of commonality between television and other media and between children and other audiences, the fields of mass communications, child development, education, psychology, and sociology can contribute to our understanding of children's interactions with television. To put the knowledge in these fields to use in understanding children's interactions with television, we need to analyze what makes television as a medium and children as an audience each simultaneously special and ordinary. We will begin the analysis with the more important parts: what makes television and children each special.

THE TELEVISION MEDIUM

The Ubiquitous Set

Everyone knows that television is an ubiquitous medium in virtually all Westernized countries. The litany of statistics for the United States is familiar. Television is in more than 95% of all American households, more common than telephones and indoor toilets. Most homes have more than one operating set. In an average residence, a set is turned on about seven hours a day. The average family member devotes two and one-half to five hours a day to viewing. At high school graduation, American children will have spent more time in front of the television set than in a classroom. By the time they are 65, more than nine full years of their lives will have been devoted to watching television.

In the 30 years since television first began to take hold in the United States, it has significantly altered politics, education, marketing, news, popular culture, social life, and family life. At the beginning of the 1950s television was in about one of every 15 American homes. By the end of the decade it was in about seven of every eight! It was adopted most rapidly by families with young children. It has changed what children and their parents do at home, what the home environment is like, where they turn for information and entertainment, and what information and entertainment are easily available to them at home and at school. Today, all children and an increasing number of adults are completely unaware of these changes. Television is an unremarkable part of their daily activities, accepted as the source of believable news, important information and education, useful product information, accurate social knowledge, pleasurable entertainment, and relaxing companionship. Most people cannot even imagine what life would be like without it.

Recent technological advances have not altered television's integral position in American life. Videogame players and personal computers have proliferated in American homes, but our best evidence indicates that the number of owners is still quite small (less than a quarter of all homes now have personal computers) and that the adoption rate is not high enough for videogame players or personal computers to saturate the home market any time soon. Some even question whether these media are attractive enough to induce most families to spend the money necessary to acquire them and support their use. Moreover, the ways in which one interacts with videogame players and personal computers and the kinds of content they deliver are quite different from those for television. Consequently, they are likely to play a different role in children's lives from that played by television. It is important to analyze that role, but it is not feasible to do so within the confines of this book (see Greenfield, 1984, for one such analysis).

Like videogame players and personal computers, cable, direct-broadcast satellite, and pay TV have also been hailed as important recent technological advances that compete with television. They have reduced restraints on the dissemination of television-like content, cut into the monopoly of the three major networks, and somewhat altered the balance of programming types offered to viewers. But unlike videogame players and personal computers, their modes of interaction and content are virtually identical to those once found exclusively on over-the-air network, independent, and public stations. For this reason the term "television" will refer to all manner of distribution systems for film and video material viewed on a television set. On a few occasions it will be important to differentiate among the systems, but otherwise "television" means program and nonprogram content distributed by "free" over-the-air broadcast, by for-a-fee over-the-air broadcast, by cable, and by direct-broadcast satellite. These distribution systems have only served to increase the ubiquity and use of a medium that was already ubiquitous and heavily used when it was only "free" over-the-air broadcasting.

Realistic Content

It is not only the ubiquity of television's distribution and use that makes it important. Equally significant is the nature of its content. Television's technological capabilities are such that it can present content that is closer to real life than is content presented by any other media except film and videodisc. The major communication codes of face-to-face interaction are used on television. We can hear what people say to each other, and we can hear and see how they use their voices, faces, hands, and bodies. If a program calls for children to visit the White House and talk with the President, television permits us to see the wonder and trepidation on their faces, their constrained gestures and clenched hands, and the care with which they enter the Oval Office. When they speak, we can listen to their words. We can also hear how quiet their voices are, how little they use intonation to emphasize words, how much they hesitate between words, and how they half laugh with embarrassment.

In addition to the linguistic, paralinguistic, facial expression, postural, and movement codes, television also uses the artifactual and spatio-temporal codes of face-to-face interaction. When we are shown the President, we will be able to see that he is dressed in a conservative but elegant suit that conveys something of his power, prestige, wealth, and exquisite taste. The understated colors that are so carefully coordinated, the fine quality of the wool, the handkerchief in his breast pocket, the monogram on the shirt, and the fine leather wing-tip shoes will all convey qualities of the presidency to us, as they do to the children visiting him. So, too, will these qualities be communicated by the furniture, flags, and decor of the room. The sequence of events during the children's visit will also be informative, as it is in everyday life. We will see if the President recognizes the discomfort of the children, if he attempts to put them at their ease, if he is able to talk with them at their level, if the children react, and if the President and the children feel comfortable at the end of the visit. We will notice how quickly or slowly the President recognizes the children's discomfort and how long he waits before putting them at ease. We can see how much distance the children place between themselves and the President when they first enter the Oval Office and if they are all clustered around his desk by the end of the visit.

The only face-to-face communication modes that are missing from television are those relying on the senses of smell and touch. Watching television, we will not smell the delicate hints of polish, flowers, and cologne in the Oval Office. We will not be able to feel the smoothness of the suit wool or the sweatiness of the children's hands. But think for a moment of how many more communication modes are unavailable when the children and the President, their actions and reactions, and the Oval Office are conveyed in a book or newspaper story, in photographs or drawings, in a radio program, in a videogame, or on a personal computer. Realize, too, that smell and touch are the two modes of communication least used in face-to-face interactions among Americans. Thus, television more than any other media except film and videodisc, and only slightly less than face-to-face interaction, provides experiences that draw upon the full range of human communication codes.

Constructed Content

If television lacks a few of the communication modes of everyday life, it probably makes up for it with a few communicative strengths that are ordinarily absent from everyday life. These strengths derive from the fact that all television content is to a greater or lesser degree constructed. It is chosen to be interesting, convey information, tell a story, educate, or persuade. An irrelevant telephone call in the middle of the visit with the President will be omitted. We may not see the President on a day when his suit is slightly outmoded or worn. The President and the children will probably have been specially coached so that the visit will be entertaining and informative for viewers. If something does not go quite right one time, they may get another chance at it or it may be edited out of the final tape. The sense of the visit may be enhanced by music, close-ups of the President's or children's faces, slow motion, or quick shifts from the children's clenched hands to the President's smiling face.

Not only entertainment programs but also news, commercials, public affairs programs, and educational programs come to us after others have carefully chosen their messages and skillfully used the technology to convey these messages in as interesting and impactful a way as possible. The creators of television content use nearly all the communication codes of face-to-face interaction and add to them filmic codes not available in everyday life. The slow fade, the quick cut, slow motion, speeded up motion, and numerous other techniques and conventions can be used to communicate the same meaning conveyed by the codes of everyday life or to augment or alter that meaning. Everyday life is rarely so deliberately or artfully constructed and conveyed as is life on television.

A Special Medium

The ubiquity, realism, and constructedness of television suggest that its contributions to modern life could be quite large, for good or ill. Here is a medium that virtually everyone uses some of the time and many people use much of the time. They like and trust it. The technological capabilities of the medium make it possible to present lifelike content the attractiveness and meaning of which can be enhanced through a variety of production techniques. Because the medium presents so many opportunities for constructing powerful messages about our physical and social world and distributing them to virtually every home and many schools in the nation, there is recurrent interest in evaluating these messages.

Everyone recognizes the potential of television for doing good and for doing ill. Not only can it inform, educate, enlighten, challenge, inspire, and enthuse, it can also deaden and misinform. Many have focused on what television does wrong. Critics complain that cartoons and prime-time programs often feature physical and verbal violence; that commercial advertising urges a misplaced and wasteful consumerism; that news entertains rather than informs; that instructional programs sugarcoat learning; and that virtually every type of content is sometimes sexist, racist, and ageist. All in all, these critics find television's representation of American life to be unbalanced and, worse yet, lacking in vision. A few cry out that television is a wonderland, as well as a wasteland, name many fine programs, and urge that we make the most of television's potential for doing good.

Now it is clear why television can be singled out. It presents lifelike experiences for viewers to enjoy and it presents them much more effectively and often than do such other communication media as radio, newspapers, books, magazines, computers, films, and comics. It may even present them more effectively and often than do such important everyday experiences as attending school, participating in social organizations, and joining in religious services and study. Its content and the way in which the content is presented have interesting parallels with and provocative differences from everyday life. More than other media, television looks as though it could deliver much that is good and bad to the American public. Television stands out from other media, which also have the potential to influence us, because it can present more lifelike content than most other media and is generally used much more than any of them. These characteristics make the medium important for everyone but especially for children whose own characteristics make them a special audience for television.

THE CHILD AUDIENCE

Sometimes wise and disconcertingly like adults, children are nonetheless children. To the wonder, joy, and vexation of adults, they are different. As they grow older, they become increasingly like us and therefore intelligible to us, but at each age or stage of development there is something for adults to learn more about, to be bemused by, and to adjust to. Where childhood begins and ends and what parts of it are relevant to the study of children and television are matters of some debate. Most of the time in this book a generic reference to "children," "child," or "childhood" will include the period from birth to the end of adolescence, but when necessary we will differentiate among infants, preschoolers, younger children, older children, younger adolescents, and older adolescents—or any subset or superordinate set of these age groups. Children in these different age groups differ from each other and from adults in many ways, but for our purposes only three are important.

Incomplete World Knowledge

One important characteristic of children is their limited knowledge of virtually all aspects of the physical and social world in which they live. All of us acquire such knowledge throughout our lives, but the most important learning usually occurs during childhood. This is the time when individuals learn what must be known if they are to function in their culture. They learn what others believe about how the physical, human, and ethereal worlds work and how to behave with the people, animals, plants, objects, ideas, and spirits in them. They become complete human beings, recognizable members of a cultural and subcultural group. But until this process is complete, children are marked by their incomplete knowledge of a world that adults around them take for granted.

Children, then, come to television knowing less about the physical and social world than do older viewers and the adults who create television content. This has several implications for children's transactions with television: (1) Children may fail to understand or may misunderstand program content if they lack the background knowledge required to understand it; (2) children may accept program content as accurate "information" when other more knowledgeable viewers know it to be otherwise; and (3) children may evaluate content without taking proper account of the means and motives for producing and broadcasting that content. Examples from my own and others' research will illustrate these possibilities.

As an example of the importance of background knowledge for correctly understanding television content, consider a *Sesame Street* segment intended to teach preschoolers about binoculars (Flagg, Housen, & Lesser, 1978). This was an animated segment featuring Thelma Thumb, a girl who could magically make herself small. In "Lost Binoculars," Thelma uses the binoculars both to magnify and to reduce images. The magpie Cyrus then flies off with the binoculars and drops them. To retrieve them, Thelma must herself become small. In this state she again shows that binoculars can both magnifiy and reduce images. Since most preschoolers do not know that binoculars are designed to magnify the images of distant objects, they believe Thelma is always playing with them, even when she uses them to examine a faraway tree where Cyrus may be. Only those preschoolers who already know binoculars' function will correctly distinguish when Thelma is just playing from when she is using the binoculars as a tool.

This same study and some of my own work illustrate how less informed children can acquire inaccurate information from television. After watching "Lost Binoculars," preschoolers who did not already know about binoculars believed that people use them for two purposes—to make things big and to make things small. In my own work (Dorr, 1980), a 7-year-old boy reported that, judging by what he had seen on television, Native Americans did not wear shirts. He was concerned because this meant they could not wear bullet-proof vests in cowboy and Indian programs and so might be harmed by the occasional real bullet that somehow appeared among television's usually fake bullets. Like the preschoolers who did not know about binoculars before watching Thelma Thumb, this little boy took seriously what television told him about Native American habits of dress and so acquired wrong information from his viewing.

Finally, let us illustrate the interpretive problems encountered by children who do not understand the means and motives for producing and broadcasting television programs and commercials (Dorr, 1980, 1983). A 9-year-old girl told us she did not have to be careful crossing the street because she could always go to the hospital, as the bionic woman did, to get replacements better than her own completely human body. Many 5-year-olds told us that commercials were very helpful because they showed what products and services were really like. All these children somewhat mistakenly granted credibility to television content that should have been treated more as fantasy or persuasion. If they had understood more about television production and about motives for producing and broadcasting different types of content, they would probably have given less credence to what they saw and been less misinformed by it.

Eagerness to Learn

The possibility that children's incomplete knowledge of their physical and social world can lead them to misunderstand, misevaluate, and wrongly learn from television is compounded by children's openness to learning. Children are notoriously curious and eager. Adults lament this characteristic when it leads children to ask endless questions, poke their fingers and noses into troublesome places, take things apart, and try out unsavory words and actions. Many believe that curiosity and the will to learn are inherent to childhood. How else, they argue, could Mother Nature ensure that each generation would learn enough, first, to survive to produce another generation and, then, to rear the young until they in turn are old enough to reproduce?

The sources of children's openness to learning (and the causes of its partial death in adolescence and adulthood) cannot be settled now, nor is it particularly important that we do so. It is important, though, to recognize that children, as television viewers and as participants in the rest of everyday life, are especially open to influence. Television offers them interesting, plausible information about the physical, social, and spiritual world they are so eager to learn about.

Different Approaches to Learning

Although eager to learn, children only gradually acquire the skills and background knowledge needed for effective and efficient learning. Compared to those of adults, young children's abilities to recognize what is important and to pick it out from other material are limited. Their attention and memory spans are short. They do not have the bag of tricks many adults can use to keep their attention from flagging and to remember things. They are not as able to attend to and understand the soundtrack, as opposed to the visual images, of television. They tend to focus on one or only a limited number of elements, even when more than that are important, and they have difficulty mentally manipulating several elements simultaneously. They do not understand many of the rules for manipulating elements. For them, several subordinate classes cannot all belong to the same superordinate class; elements cannot be multiply classified according to several categories and hierarchies; many reversible processes (e.g., changing the shape of a ball of clay) cannot be reversed; and visual alterations in materials are wrongly associated with alterations in other qualities of the materials (e.g., changing the clay's shape changes its weight).

The differences between children and adults change and usually diminish as children develop. But children of all ages are to some extent different from adults in the ways in which they attend to, process, remember, and use television content. These age-related qualitative differences in children's thinking and learning are the third characteristic of children that is important for this book.

A Special Audience

So, here we have children lacking knowledge of their physical and social world, eager to learn about it, and only partially equipped with the needed learning tools. These characteristics make children a markedly different mass media audience (and participant in everyday life) than are adults. Adults too can be uninformed or misinformed, eager to learn, and inadequate learners, but these characteristics are much less generally and frequently found in adult viewers. One can count on children to know less about most topics, to be more interested in learning about many things, and to be more restricted in their ability to understand and learn. That makes them an interesting focus of study. What we learn can be used to nurture, instruct, and socialize children so that they become productive, supportive members of our culture, able in their turn to produce and rear another generation of productive, supportive people.

COMMONALITIES AMONG MEDIA AND AMONG AUDIENCES

Any analysis of the nature of the television medium and of the child audience leads immediately to a recognition of the commonalities between children and other audiences and between television and other media. For students of communication, education, psychology, child development, and sociology it is as important to recognize these commonalities as it is to know how children and television are unique. When one recognizes the commonalities, one's knowledge expands exponentially. What one knows about adults, about other media, and about children apart from television becomes relevant to one's consideration of children and television.

Television and Other Media

Several important variables can be identified as the basis for comparing media. These include the number and types of communication codes used, how analogue or digital the medium is, how interruptible and repeatable the content presentation is, how transportable the medium is, how much the content is aimed at a mass or targeted audience, the types of content typically presented, the extent to which the service must be directly paid for, and the economic and regulatory structures within which the medium functions. It is an intellectually challenging task to establish what variables are important for comparing media and why, but the utility of doing so is obvious. With such a scheme one can more clearly see how and how much television is like and unlike other media and so better understand its roles as one medium among many in children's lives.

As a purveyor of popular culture, a means of educating and informing, and a vehicle for advertising, television has important connections to several other media. Films and books are the inspirations for television programs; theatrical films later appear on television; television personalities and programs are featured in magazines and newspapers; news magazines, newspapers, the radio, and television programs carry the same news and use each other as news sources; educational films become instructional television programs; television programs are advertised on radio and in newspapers and magazines; radio stations, magazines, films, newspapers, videogames, and personal computers are advertised on television; and an advertising campaign for a product or service is simultaneously conducted over television, radio, and magazines. The commercial broadcasting system developed directly from the commercial radio networks, but today television is most similar to film in terms of the communication codes used, the storytelling emphasis, the narrative form, the dramatic conventions, the popular culture orientation, and the national distribution. Thus, there are commonalities between television and film and radio specifically and between television and all other purveyors of popular culture, information, education, and advertising that make other media research pertinent to understanding the role of television in children's lives.

Children and Other Audiences

Just as media can be compared along important dimensions, so too can children be compared among themselves and to adults. Knowledge of the physical and social world, curiosity and interest in learning, and learning processes were earlier singled out as three characteristics of children that are most important for this book. On the first two dimensions, children can be said to increase and decrease respectively as they mature into adults. The third dimension, learning processes, needs to be broken into several component parts, as we will do in a subsequent chapter, before it becomes a useful basis for comparing children among themselves and to adults.

The greatest similarity between children of different ages and between children and adults is in the communicative, psychological, and social tasks they perform daily. Broadly speaking, they must all make sense of their experiences and learn from or adapt to them enough to continue living. Herein lie several focal problems in communication, education, psychology, and sociology, problems that arise for adults and children both. They include how any particular experience is influenced by an individual's idealized models of that type of situation; how information processing styles and abilities influence what is attended to, remembered, or utilized; how to characterize the social circumstances under which adaptation is great enough that we deem it to be socialization, social influence, or education; and how one's knowledge of the goals of those creating or participating in a situation influences one's understanding of and reaction to the situation.

Children and adults being what they are, the processes by which these several communicative, psychological, and social tasks occur are likely to be more obvious in children's thoughts, behaviors, and reactions and more subtle in those of adults. Children, then, can provide clearer demonstrations of these processes in action. On the other hand, adults are often a more tractable population to study. Because researchers are adults, they usually understand adults better than children. Moreover, adults are usually more aware of their own internal processes and more able to describe what they think, feel, know, believe, understand, have done, and will do. So, although phenomena are often more subtle with adults, it is easier with them to select and successfully carry out appropriate experimental procedures. Thus, children and adults offer different advantages as research participants. Choosing the easier group for any given study more rapidly enhances understanding of the communicative, psychological, and social tasks commonly faced by both children and adults.

Ordinary Children and Television

These points of commonality between television and other media and between children and other audience members have led some to question the merit of singling out children's transactions with television as an area for study (see an interesting historical analysis by the communications researchers Byron Reeves and Ellen Wartella, 1985). A small but articulate group of scholars has identified similarities between television today and radio, comics, and movies in the past and between television today and film today and concluded that the study of television belongs only within the study of mass media per se. Others have argued that children's transactions with television do not differ in any substantive way from the transactions of other viewers with television. The same processes occur for all viewers, they say, even if they differ in amount.

There is some legitimacy to these claims but not enough to warrant complete disregard for the study of children's transactions with television. There are points of similarity between television and other media and between children and other audiences, but there are also the very important differences described earlier in the chapter. Throughout this book we will walk a tightrope between these two perspectives: "children and television" as a topic unto itself and "children and television" as an interesting special case in the fields of mass communication, psychology, child development, education, and sociology. Doing so will enable us to learn the most possible about how children use and are affected by television.

BOOBS, BRAINS, MAGIC WINDOWS, AND IDIOT BOXES

Everyone living in the United States today has an opinion about television's value and about the intelligence of the children who use it. We all know the medium and its offerings well, and we all know what we and our friends did with television while we were growing up. Some of us even know what children in our homes or communities do with television today. These everyday experiences make everyone experts about children's transactions with television and lead us, as they have led other experts, to fervently held, polarized opinions.

Opinions about television can be rather negative. Most people see the power of television to do harm or, at least, to promote mediocrity. They recognize that the ubiquity, realism, and constructed nature of television content give it a special place in American life and decry the pap, drivel, misinformation, twisted values, and dangerous ideas it dispenses. For them television becomes the idiot box, the boob tube, the seducer, the hypnotist. A few people adopt a more positive attitude to television, emphasizing the important, worthwhile education, information, attitudes, and behaviors this powerful medium can convey. For them television becomes a magic window, a master teacher, a window on the world, a ticket to the best of everything.

Opinions about the viewing public are usually rather contradictory. When referring to how others use television, opinions are generally negative. Too many people, including children, seem to watch television instead of doing better things with their time and, even worse, to watch mediocre or awful programs. And children, in their eagerness to learn about a world they imperfectly understand, seem far too ready to accept what television tells them and to put it into practice. They are seen as boobs, zombies, couch potatoes, and slavish imitators who need to straighten up and fly right.

Opinions about oneself as a member of the viewing public are often amazingly different. Somehow one's own television viewing is mostly fine, either because one watches good programs and not too many of them or because one uses television for just exactly the right amount of relaxation and entertainment. Moreover, one is living proof that children, especially children like oneself, are smart about television. "After all," one says, "I turned out just fine. That must mean that I was able to make sense of television, use whatever good stuff it gave me, and forget the rest." Here, then, the viewer becomes a brain, using television well to provide the right mix of entertainment and enlightenment and responsibly picking and choosing the right television messages to accept and reject.

It is easy for television to seem like an idiot box or a magic window and for child viewers to seem like boobs or brains. The power of the medium, the diversity of its content, the abilities of children, the diversity among them, and the many different things any one child does all provide ample support for any complimentary or uncomplimentary opinion. Because we have all been children and are all still television viewers, we have already developed our own opinions about television and children. These opinions, developed through experiences in everyday life, can and should be reexamined in light of what has been learned from three decades of research. One soon sees that both children and television are neither as good nor as bad as thinking would have them be and learns how to maximize the magic of television and the braininess of the children using it.

2

MAKING SENSE OF TELEVISION

Although people often agree about the messages and concrete details of television content, each viewer must himself or herself engage in information-processing, interpretive, and evaluative activities in order to determine what has been seen and what it means.

Television sends out sights and sounds to viewers who decide for themselves what to make of these stimuli. Those who create television content decide what messages they want to send. In the final analysis, however, these are not the messages viewers *receive*, rather they are the messages viewers *interpret*. Viewers' interpretations then become television's messages for all intents and purposes. By what principles and processes do child and adult viewers carry out their interpretive tasks, constructing meaning from the visual and auditory stimuli television provides for them? And what does it mean to say that meaning is constructed?

A CONSTRUCTIVIST PERSPECTIVE

The constructivist perspective affirms that an individual selects and interprets the raw materials of experience to produce his or her own understanding of what that experience is. Physical reality is not denied; there are objects, people, animals, sounds, words, and events everywhere in life. But what is attended to and what is dismissed, what is considered important and what unimportant, how elements are organized into categories and hierarchies, and what meaning is attached to any physical reality are all determined by the individual. The active work that must be done in order to make sense of experience, this social construction of reality (Berger & Luckmann, 1966), ultimately transforms even physical reality into different realities for different peoples.

An informative illustration of these ideas can be found in how different people deal with color. Science tells us that visible light contains continuously changing color determined by the wavelength of the light, that the color of any object is determined by the wavelengths of light it absorbs and those it reflects, and that the human visual system can register all wavelengths of visible light. Yet, in their everyday lives, people do not treat color this way.

Every culture divides the spectrum into sections, giving each a color name, and these sections differ from culture to culture. Our biggest sections are called red, yellow, blue, and green and, of course, white and black. Very small sections are identified by names such as turquoise, eggshell blue, and navy. For us, these are the "real colors" of the world, but not so for some other peoples. One culture, for instance, has two major color categories, colors of living and of dead plants, while another has no yellow or orange as we know them but rather a color whose wavelength falls between our two. For these peoples, *their* colors not ours are the real colors of the world. The physical reality is that virtually all colors exist in everyone's world and can be received by everyone's visual system, but the constructed—and socially significant—reality is that different people's worlds are made up of different colors.

The differing social constructions of the world of color are but an extreme example of the fact that the reality with which people operate every day is one they themselves fashion. Each person uses available physical stimuli, the human physiological apparatus, and the information-processing systems and interpretive schemes taught by his or her culture to interact with and make sense of the world moment by moment day by day for every experience. In this respect interacting with television and its content is no different from any other experience in life. Each and every viewer constructs meaning for programs and commericals that were created by people who used the technology and their own cultural knowledge to put meaning into the content in the first place.

Children Constructing Meaning

A constructivist position, at least a mild version of it, comes naturally to those studying children. Because children do not know as much about the world as adults do and because they are still learning how to process and use information, children regularly fail to understand or use program content in ways adults would. These "failures" make it immediately apparent that the child viewer must do active work to watch television, make sense of its content, and utilize "its" messages. A child watches a superhero running in slow motion with special sound effects and asks how he will ever catch the villains when he is running so slowly. This child is obviously engaged in an active process of making sense of the program and, just as obviously, is not using some available program "information" to interpret it as the program creators intended and as other more knowledgeable viewers would interpret it. What better evidence does anyone need that viewers must construct meaning for television programs?

Some of the earliest research on children and television recognized that people play an important part in determining what any experience means for them. In studying the introduction of television to American and Canadian children, one of the founding fathers of communications, Wilbur Schramm, and two of his colleagues put it this way:

> In a sense the term "effect" is misleading because it suggests that television "does something" to children. The connotation is that television is the actor, the children are acted upon. Children are thus made to seem relatively inert; television, relatively active. Children are sitting victims; television bites them. Nothing can be further from the fact. It is the children who are most active in this relationship. It is they who use television, rather than television that uses them. (Schramm, Lyle, & Parker, 1961, p. 1)

English researchers studying the new medium of television also recognized that different children might find different meanings in the same content. For instance, they thought that adolescent girls closer to marriageable age would find British soap operas more meaningful than would younger adolescent girls, even though girls of both ages watched the soaps equally often. Indeed, older girls took the doleful soap opera view of love and marriage to heart and were more pessimistic than younger girls about their prospects for happy male-female relationships (Himmelweit et al., 1958).

Ever since these earliest explorations of the meaning of television for children's lives, many of those studying children and television—particularly those taking a developmental perspective—have recognized that television stimuli must be interpreted and utilized by viewers. Children are not empty vessels simply waiting to be filled up by television. They may seem quiet, even passive, while watching television, but inactive bodies do not necessarily mean inactive minds.

Social Scientists Constructing Meaning

In mass media studies, even those involving children, researchers have often taken their own constructed meanings for television content as the standard. The message they understand to be emanating from the medium is "the message." It is easy to see why this would happen. Researchers are experts, and the opinions of experts are generally considered to be accurate. Researchers are also members of our culture, and there is considerable agreement in the messages fully socialized members of the same culture derive from the same cultural product. Finally, researchers are adults, and—at least when interacting with children—adults are considered more able to construct accurate meaning than are children.

Researchers are, however, also human beings subject to the same requirements as every other human being. They, too, must construct messages using their own unique set of past experiences, information-processing tools, and interpretive abilities. Just as we have come to recognize that children's "errors" in making sense of television content are indicative of *children's* constructive processes at work, so must we also realize that the sense researchers make of television content is similarly indicative of *researchers'* constructive processes at work.

In a biting critique of much research on children and television, the communications scholar James Anderson (1981) raised just this issue. He acknowledged that social scientists "may be moving toward the notion that messages are *constructed* from content not *delivered* by content" (p. 398), but he nonetheless criticized much of their work for its continued assumption that the meaning researchers construct for television content is the same as that constructed by viewers.

Ardent constructivists such as Anderson argue that researchers must take the time to find out what meaning each audience member, himself or herself, constructs for each piece of television content. Moreover, they assume that there may be little overlap in the meanings different viewers construct for the same content. Since uses, gratifications, and effects follow from these viewer-constructed meanings, the implications of Anderson's ardent constructivism for mass communication research are, as he notes, "startling." For everyone else studying children's transactions with television, his position impels a reexamination of the theoretical accuracy and practical utility of their notions of constructivism.

Too Much Constructivism

Currently most students of children's transactions with television agree that each viewer constructs meaning from television content, while simultaneously assuming that viewers on average construct the same meaning for the same content. A few scholars, such as James Anderson, seem to assume that there is little or no commonality in the meanings different viewers construct for the same content. For those interested in understanding television's place in children's lives, there are both theoretical and practical drawbacks to adopting a position such as this.

Good theory generally makes intuitive sense and accounts well for phenomena as they are encountered in everyday life. A constructivist perspective that puts great emphasis on meanings each individual constructs for the same content runs the risk of failing to account for the indisputable fact that very often there is substantial agreement across individuals in the meanings they have constructed.

If *Snow White* is broadcast on television, the same combinations of auditory and visual stimuli go to every viewer. Those who created *Snow White* arrived at some consensual understanding of what meanings these stimuli were going to transmit. If a viewer of *Snow White* comes from the same culture as its creators, there is a restricted range of constructed meanings that one expects from him or her. The beautiful, homebody princess would not be described as though she were an adventurous, sarcastic Princess Leia, a beleagured Cinderella, a curvaceous Wonder Woman with superhuman powers, or the ever youthful flying boy Peter Pan. If Snow White were described in any of these ways, we would not interpret the description as "normal" constructed meaning. Rather we would ask if the viewer had really watched *Snow White,* if the viewer understood our question, if he or she were crazy, or if he or she were just pulling our collective leg.

One view of the constructivist perspective puts little emphasis on the consensual meanings program creators, broadcasters, and viewers alike construct for any given piece of television content. Its adherents rightly remind us that meaning must be constructed by each participant in the mass communication situation and that there is always some important variability in meanings constructed by different people. For those interested in children and television, however, it is every bit as important to have viable theories to account for how children construct meaning that relates in identifiable ways to the common meaning a host of other child viewers, adult viewers, or adult programmers would construct for the same content. That is, the consensualities in the meanings constructed by identifiable groups of people are every bit as important to us theoretically as is the uniqueness of each person's constructed meaning. After all, one central task of childhood is learning enough about the physical and social world and about how to process and interpret raw experience so that you can share a world with adults and other children.

The practical drawback to focusing solely on individuals' constructions of meaning for television content should be obvious. As a mass medium, television signals are transmitted equally to thousands and even millions of sets each day. If these signals are to be useful to viewers or even just not harmful, producers and broadcasters must be able to identify the messages that viewers will find in the signals. The relevant viewers may be a culturally defined subset of the entire audience, for example, preschoolers or women or Japanese Americans, but the subset must be large, demographically identifiable, and largely in agreement about constructed meaning. When a set of viewers and their constructive tendencies can be identified, then and only then will producers and broadcasters know how to create and distribute content these viewers will enjoy, learn from, and value.

Thus there are both practical and theoretical reasons for eschewing an interpretation of the constructivist position that focuses exclusively on an individual's constructions of meaning. Such an interpretation leads us away from the theoretically interesting questions of how consensual meaning is achieved and of how culture operates to provide individuals with the tools and knowledge needed to construct meaning. It also leaves the production and broadcasting industries with little or no grounds for determining what constitutes responsible action. There is, then, a clear need for understanding how an individual constructs meaning that is shared by other members of his or her culture and for a constructivist perspective that allows for commonalities in constructed meaning.

Too Little Constructivism

In urging a position that includes a concern for consensus in interpreted meaning, one encounters relatively few problems when the focus is on the construction of "factual meaning" by well-socialized members of a shared culture. Even for children, the less well-socialized members of the culture, we can comfortably couch any idiosyncratic meanings in a framework that posits there would be shared meanings among more fully socialized cultural members. The most individualistic constructivist would agree that one can rightly expect significant commonalities in well-socialized viewers' understandings of who the television characters are, how they are dressed, where they are, and what they do.

Problems arise as soon as one moves beyond the most literal descriptions of content that was completely depicted visually and/or auditorally. Inferences about events that are implied but not depicted, attributions of motives or feelings to characters, and determinations of a program's theme require more complex cognitive processing than do literal descriptions, and they require the use of knowledge from outside the program itself. Depending on how a program is written, even adult viewers of a crime drama may disagree about whether the hero's reason for using force is to capture the villain, vent his anger and disgust, or set an example for other villains. And they may argue about the theme: One sees the program as showing that crime does not pay; another, that might makes right; and a third, that cooperation pays off. If even well-socialized adults vary in the meanings they construct in these areas, imagine the likely individual variation among children who do not know as much about the physical and social world or about the "proper" procedures for constructing meaning in all these areas.

There is likely to be even more individual variation among both children and adults in how any character, action, theme, or programming purpose is evaluated or reacted to. Even people who agree that a program theme was "cooperation pays off" may disagree in their endorsement of the theme. One person argues that the best way to get ahead in this world is always to put oneself first, to watch out for number one, to be assertive and self-protective first and foremost. Another argues that when everyone cooperates, everyone wins. Yet another argues that one's evaluation of the theme should depend on who is cooperating for what purpose. To the extent that evaluative reactions are part of the meaning constructed for any content, there are sure to be many differences in interpreted meaning across American viewers. Thus, we cannot go too far in arguing for an emphasis on consensual meaning.

The Middle Ground

We need to find a middle ground built on the fundamental assumption that each viewer must himself or herself construct meaning anew for each bit of television content viewed. It must recognize that meaning is constructed at several levels and that each matters for what children do with television. At the same time we need to remember that each individual constructor has access to the same television signals. When viewers share a common culture, they then also share a similar set of construction tools and processes for interpreting these signals. An understanding of the significance of television to children's lives must be built on an understanding of these processes by which children construct both idiosyncratic and shared meaning for television content.

CONSTRUCTIVE PROCESSES

The process of constructing meaning for television content in everyday life differs in important ways from what must be done to explain this process in a book. Ordinarily, the construction of meaning is an out-of-awareness process. It operates simultaneously on several different levels of meaning, with the levels being at once independent and interdependent. Describing the construction of meaning at any level requires making the process explicit and adopting an analytic, compartmentalized, sequential approach to presenting its components. In this book the tasks that go on as viewers construct meaning for television content will be grouped into three types, information processing, interpretation, and evaluation, that will be described in that order. Such labels, sections, orderings, and explications are essential to this book, but they should not mislead a reader into believing that the constructive process itself involves anything other than interconnected tasks that usually occur without the viewer being conscious of them.

Information-processing, interpretive, and evaluative activities all occur at one time or another in the course of making sense of television content. Information-processing activities lead to the extraction of concrete and literal meaning for television content. They involve choosing among and acting upon the auditory and visual stimuli provided by television without going beyond them. Interpretive activities go beyond these "facts" to supply content that is suggested but not actually depicted, to understand feelings and motives, and to string together pieces of content to form a larger whole. Because they go beyond the momentary physical signals of television, interpretive activities in a sense create meaning, connecting the bare bones of a skeleton together to form a structure and adding flesh, guts, and hide to make the bones into a whole creature. Evaluative activities add feelings and reactions to denotative and connotative, explicit and implicit, meaning. They involve creating pro or con, liking or disliking, involved or uninvolved relationships with content. At their most formal they may be considered attitudes, but at a less formal level they are a portion of the meaning given to any content and they play a part in determining how the other constructive activities are themselves carried out.

Information Processing

To extract a message from television content a viewer must at a minimum pick up auditory and/or visual signals from the set, send them to the brain, decode them, and place them in memory to refer to later. All these activities fall into the category of information processing and must be carried out continuously while a child is watching television. Even a typical 30-second commercial advertisement for action figures (e.g., He-Man, She-Ra, Batman, GI Joe, Wonder Woman, Mr. T) will include more "information" than a child can process at one time. Several action figures will engage in exciting battles or daring feats; there will be much movement on the screen, several different camera angles, and many quick scene changes; the soundtrack will describe the events, extoll the virtues of the dolls, and carry lively music and gripping sound effects; at some time a disclaimer "Action figures sold separately" may be printed at the bottom of the screen and the narrator may also say this. No child can look at, listen to, transmit, decode, and remember every element of such a commercial, nor will many children even choose to try—nor should they.

There are many information-processing choices and chores the child viewer faces. Physiologically, humans cannot turn off their ears very well. Children will more or less hear whatever sounds are broadcast. They can, however, make some choices about how much sound to transmit and more choices about how much to decode and store. The same choices can be made for the sights of television, but here children can also choose what to look at in the first place. In fact, most often they must choose, because too much visual material is presented in too short a time for a viewer to look at it all. This may seem counterintuitive, since most of us find it easy to see what we want to see of television's visual stimuli. However, the television screen is usually full of more images than can be scanned in the time available before the scene or camera angle changes. Because we adults generally know which images are important, we look at these without any conscious effort, pay little attention to the rest, and do not experience any sense of having to choose from among a wealth of potentially equally significant visual information. Nonetheless, we have usually made such choices, just as children make them.

Having chosen which content to pick up and send to the brain, the child still has decoding activities to engage in. The child could "correctly" recognize the visual image of She-Ra as a woman, a toy, an action figure, or She-Ra or "incorrectly" recognize it as Wonder Woman, He-Man's mother, or a cartoon character. The child could decide what action Mr. T and the rest of the A-Team figures were involved in—a fight, a rescue, a joke, an escape—and where the action was taking place. The child could determine that the words printed at the bottom of the screen mean that the figures in the commercial are not sold together as one purchase. All these decoding activities involve establishing meaning for content that was explicitly and completely presented by television without adding meaning only suggested by that content.

At some point the child will also decide what content to store in long-term memory and in what form to store it. Will a visual image be stored as is or will it be recoded into a meaningful linguistic representation such as "She-Ra?" Will anything at all be stored? If something is to be stored in memory, then the necessary mental work must be done just as it must be done for decoding. The choice whether to lay anything down, the decision about the form of the memory trace, and the process of laying something down in memory usually happen without the viewer being aware of them; nonetheless, they occur and play a part, along with picking signals, transmitting them to the brain, and decoding them, in the viewer's construction of meaning for any television content.

Several factors can influence what stimuli are attended to and processed. Some are probably built into humans: for instance, looking at faces more than at other parts of the body, looking at movement more than at stationary objects, and visually and posturally orienting toward the source of new, different, or unexpected sound. Others are learned and then carried out rather automatically: for instance, paying attention to the words of a song and looking for clues to people's motives. Still others are at least partially determined by interpretive and evaluative meanings constructed by the viewer: for instance, paying close attention to a newcaster's messages about a political candidate because one attributes objectivity to news and disregarding action figures ads because one prefers girls' toys.

In recent years there has been a burst of research showing that people learn principles and structures that guide and support their information-processing activities. The psychologist Daniel Anderson has suggested that children as young as three guide when and how much they look at the television screen at least partially by how understandable the material is likely to be (Anderson & Lorch, 1983). From repeated viewing of preschool programs children seem to have decided that incomprehensible content is likely to be associated with such features as men's voices, extended zooms and pans, and eye contact, while comprehensible content is likely to be associated with such features as women, children, and puppets (Alwitt, Anderson, Lorch, & Levin, 1980). Daniel Anderson believes that this knowledge operates as a schema for the television viewing activity.

Schemas, or schematas, are abstract knowledge structures, prototypes, ideal forms, or idealized models, if you will. They provide an internal structure for the selection and storage of content, generate expectations about that content, influence recollections of that content, and develop and change according to experience. They come in several different forms. An "action schema," for instance, involves a set of idealized expectations for a single act such as reading a book or getting arrested. A "story schema" involves a prototypical structure for a narrative: the problem, characters' feelings about it, attempts to resolve it, the outcome, and reactions to it. A "script" is a conceptual representation of a stereotyped event sequence such as having a birthday party or attending a class. Any of these schemas and more could play an important role in the information-processing activities described here and in the interpretive activities described in the next section.

When a child encounters a host of visual and auditory stimuli, schemas can be used to guide the child's choices about what stimuli to attend to and which to send to the brain. If the child decides a story is about a girl's birthday party and has birthday party schemas, then the child knows to look and listen for cake and ice cream, presents, games or other entertainment, guests, and the person whose birthday it is. The child can usually safely ignore furniture in the room, adults who bring the child guests, pets, other food, and off-hand conversations among guests. If pin-the-tail-on-the-donkey is played, the child may call up an action schema to guide attention *to* the blindfold over the eyes, the child's hand holding the tail, and the adult's hands spinning the child and *away from* the room in which the game is played, the child's clothes, and the adult's gender. If the child has a script for birthday parties, then he or she also knows something about the order in which to expect the elements and events to appear and can be mentally prepared to attend to them. Schemas such as these can also help decoding; the child, for instance, knows there should be something in the television content that can be decoded to be the cake. And they can guide storage in memory; the child already has an idealized structure into which can be slotted the particular elements and events of this birthday party.

It is easy to see from the birthday party example how important schemas can be for the information-processing activities involved in making sense of television content, but they are not the only influences on the process. Viewer needs and interests, their abilities and training, their innate information-processing patterns, their interpretations and evaluations of content, and the characteristics of the content itself can all at one time or another influence what stimuli are attended to, transmitted to the brain, decoded, and stored in memory as part of the process of making sense of television content.

Interpretation

Interpretive activities in the construction of meaning go beyond selecting, decoding, and remembering physical stimuli to processes that put together groups of stimuli and that lead to conclusions about "content" that is implied but never directly stated or shown. They require viewers to use schemas and other experience-based knowledge about what people are like, how things work, and the normal course of events to decide what content elements to relate to each other, what events must have occurred even though they were not depicted, and what feelings and motives were experienced by the television characters and those who created and broadcast the television content. These three types of decisions, or activities, will be referred to respectively as integration, inference, and attribution. Together they make up the interpretive activities in which viewers may engage in order to make sense of television content.

Television content varies in the extent to which viewers need to attribute, infer, or integrate in order to construct meanings like those the creators had in mind, and viewers vary among themselves and from time to time in their abilities and inclinations to engage in attribution, inference, and integration. As we examine each interpretive process more closely, we will choose as illustration television content that requires substantial interpretation. Moreover, we will take as our standard the ways in which well-socialized but average American adult viewers would make sense of this content when they were inclined to put all their constructive processes to work. With such content and viewers as the point of departure, we will have a good basis for understanding some of the challenges child viewers can face in interpreting television content.

Attributions are the explanations a viewer develops for why someone does something, the decisions he or she makes about how someone is feeling, and the conclusions he or she reaches about the inherent qualities of people or animals. A viewer is making attributions when he or she decides that the hero is pretending to be a derelict because he wants to catch the villain, that Walter Cronkite is feeling excited about the space launch, or that Donald Duck is irascible.

The term "attribution" is now fairly common in the research literature. It is used specifically to refer to people's ascriptions of internal states, traits, and motives to other people, animals, or anthropomorphized objects. In everyday English we might call these ascriptions "inferences." The research literature being as it is, we will reserve the term "inferences" for those times when one decides that events that have not been depicted should nonetheless be understood to have occurred.

Let us explore attributional processes and the world knowledge they may require the viewer to use. In a segment of *Sesame Street* a mummy in the depths of an Egyptian pyramid starts to sing and dance in front of Ernie who shakes and yells "Bert!" in a quavery voice. Viewers may decide that Ernie is afraid. To make this attribution they may refer to what they know about how people deal with fear—a shaking body, a quavery voice, and a quick call for help are all common signs of fear. They may or may not also refer to their knowledge of when people feel afraid and of how timorous a person Ernie is.

Suppose Ernie was neither seen nor heard while the mummy was singing and dancing, but it had been established that Ernie was off-camera watching the mummy's performance. In order to attribute fear to Ernie in this segment, viewers would have to draw upon some knowledge other than how people express fear. They could remember that Egyptian tombs are mysterious, that mummies cannot move or speak, that most people would feel some trepidation in a tomb, that nearly everyone would become afraid at unexpected sounds or movements in the tomb, and/or that Ernie is a character who is more likely to be fearful than intrepid. For children it is more difficult to attribute fear to Ernie in the second than in the first example, but in both examples viewers must refer to knowledge not contained in the program itself if they are to attribute fear to Ernie. Depending on the knowledge needed, such attributions may be easy, hard, or impossible for children.

Because we are talking about television, there is one attribution that can be especially important in making sense of its content. It is attributing purposes or motives to those who created and broadcast the content. If viewers attribute the goal of helping children to those responsible for *Mister Rogers' Neighborhood*, then they may construct somewhat different meaning for its content than they would if they believed its goal was to attract the largest possible audience or to sell a product. Similarly, if children believe the action figure commercial described earlier was intended to keep them up-to-date on the latest products, they will probably take its content more seriously than if they believe it was intended to convince them to part with some of their money. Because different types of television content are produced for different reasons with correspondingly different standards for accuracy, balance, pleasure, and redeeming social value, attributing motives to those who created the content can have important ramifications for the sense made of it.

The process of making inferences, as defined here, involves deciding that events that have not been shown should still be thought of as having occurred. As such, inference making always requires that one refer to one's storehouse of knowledge, be it accurate or inaccurate knowledge. Think for a moment about what one may know about romantic love: its existence, the sex and age of those who usually experience it, the number of people feeling it for each other at any one time, how it can be expressed, where it can be expressed, and the symbols we have for representing it. Knowledge such as this may be used to infer how romantic love will be expressed when a husband and wife have a candlelit dinner at home and then go arm in arm to the bedroom, turning out the light, and shutting the door.

Children, who lack the background knowledge adults have about romantic love, will not make such inferences. Jerzy Kosinski (1970) used this fact about children (and people of every age) to humorous advantage in his novel *Being There*. His character, Chance, has no opportunity as he is growing up to learn everything one usually learns about romantic love. Chance's only socialization experiences are working in a garden, where there is no romantic love, and watching television, where only some aspects of romantic love are explicitly depicted. When Chance has grown to manhood, he is inadvertently thrust into society. He mystifies women by being attentive, hugging and kissing them, and even getting into bed with one or two, without ever going any further. He goes just as far as shown on television. As he grew up, Chance never learned enough about sexual behavior to understand when some sexual activities, while not literally depicted on the screen, were still intended to be part of a television story. Like Chance, most viewers occasionally fail to know enough to infer events that are not depicted. Depending on what they watch, younger viewers may often fail at inference making.

Attribution and inference, as is evident from the discussion, ordinarily involve integrating together simultaneous or sequential elements of television content. One may attribute fear to Ernie solely on the basis of his shaking body, but the attribution is much better made referring to his shaking body *and* his quavery voice *and* his presence in a dimly lit, unusual environment *and* the mummy's singing and dancing *and* Ernie's quick call for Bert just as soon as the mummy begins to perform. Similarly one could perhaps infer that the husband and wife will have intercourse because they are having a nice dinner together, but the inference is much better made referring to the dinner *and* their relationship to each other *and* their physical contact when they leave the dinner table *and* their entrance into the bedroom *and* their turning out the light *and* the slow shutting of the door. Thus, the third interpretive activity, integration, is essential to the other two.

Even when television content is produced so that there is no real need to supply "missing" motives, feelings, or events, constructing meaning for it usually involves integrating together several simultaneous or sequential elements. To decide that a heroine is chasing a villain the viewer may need to integrate the scene that established that the fleeing person is indeed the villain with the scene that established that the chasing person is indeed the heroine with the chase scene itself. To decide that a villain is in jail a viewer may need to integrate the man's striped work shirt and pants, the small room he is in, the fold-down cot he sits on, and the open toilet bowl in a nearby corner. To decide that the theme of a *Feeling Free* episode is that handicapped and nonhandicapped children can be friends, a viewer may need to integrate early scenes of the children playing separately with later scenes of them seeking out activities they both enjoy with final scenes of the two children engrossed in joint play.

Schemas, those abstract knowledge structures described in the earlier section on information-processing activities, can also be helpful when viewers engage in interpretive activities. A story schema is a ready guide for which pieces of television content to integrate together to determine what the story is about. Scripts, too, can be helpful in choosing content for integrative activities. And both scripts and schemas can be used to infer content that was not explicitly presented. If two characters are shown entering a restaurant, sitting down at a table, perusing a menu, hatching a plot over aperitifs, and then leaving the restaurant deep in discussion, a restaurant script leads easily to the inference that the characters ordered meals, ate them, paid the bills, and tipped the waitress, even though these events were never shown.

Integration, attribution, and inference are all processes that can be brought into play to construct meaning from physical stimuli. One can think that information processing occurs first and that the processed information is then integrated together and/or used to make inferences and attribute motives, purposes, and feelings. Roughly speaking, this is a useful but somewhat inaccurate model. While integration, attribution, and inference can occur after information processing, they can also occur during and even in some senses before information processing. What is processed and how it is processed are demonstrably intertwined with interpretive processes, as some of the examples in this section should make clear. Having attributed fear to Ernie or irascibility to Donald, for instance, a viewer may be especially attentive to subsequent content that confirms these attributions. Constructing meaning now looks rather like Janus, the two-faced god of old, but even this image is inadequate since it does not include the evaluative activities that are also a part of constructing meaning for television content.

Evaluation

In evaluative activities children react to what they view. They feel as well as think. They laugh, cry, get scared or angry, approve or disapprove. They attach positive and negative valences to the content they have been processing and interpreting, decide whom they admire and whom they loathe, judge the morality of the actions they see, and assign worth to the motives of those who produce and broadcast each program and commercial.

Most emphasis in everyday life, as well as in television research and production, is on getting the message rather than on feelings about the message. The focus is how people make sense of what they experience, how they come to understand the content delivered by a newspaper or a television program. With children, an additional interest is how they learn to make sense of experience as adults do and to communicate so that others will understand them. But humans are not simply rational machines, using a knowledge base and a set of rules to construct literal and figurative meaning for their experiences. Humans are creatures with feelings—interest, disinterest, distaste, boredom, ennui, enthusiasm, fear, anger, and joy—as well as thoughts. And they judge experiences and people and place value upon them.

Evaluative activities are not obligatory in the same sense that information-processing and interpretive activities are. Those who produce television content and those who watch it share the belief that there are messages in that content, that the creators' job is to make the messages accessible to the viewers, and that the viewers' job is to find the correct or intended messages in the content. Viewers must engage in information-processing and interpretive activities if they are to do their job. No one assumes that viewers must also have feelings about the content, nor do they assume—as they do with television messages—that a correct set or sequence of feelings can be specified for each piece of television content. A set of inappropriate feelings can be specified; for example, no one should feel glad when the hero suffers great pain. Yet a standard for correct feelings cannot be established in the same way that a standard for correct messages can. This makes it difficult to regard evaluative activities as tasks aimed at achieving certain goals.

Emotional responses to television content can occur with little or no thought by the viewer. Some depictions such as a horrible monster, a baby cuddled by its adoring father, a man being strangled, or a cavorting puppy are emotionally evocative simply because in everyday life feelings are associated with these events. The emotional responses of protagonists can also be evocative. Seeing a character who very clearly shows feelings of disgust, guilt, amusement, or joy can evoke similar feelings in the viewer. Among those who study emotions there are serious disagreements about how much certain stimuli, events, or expressions of emotion are recognized and/or responded to automatically, without any learning having occurred. No one, however, doubts that recognizing emotions and associating certain emotions with certain stimuli can both be learned and become automatic. In some circumstances, then, child viewers need only attend to what is being presented on television in order to produce emotional responses without any further thought.

Other emotional responses to television content involve more mental activity during viewing. Often, for instance, a character does not show what he or she is feeling, or the character is not even on the screen. To have feelings like those of the character the viewer must think about what the character is like, what the character's goals are, what the situation is like, and/or what events led up to the situation, use this information to infer the character's feelings, and then have similar feelings himself or herself. The likelihood of having such similar feelings increases when children like and admire a character. When they do not like or respect a character, any feelings they have are likely to be opposite to those of the character. If the character is suffering, they will be happy; if the character is reaping rewards, they will be sad or mad.

Anticipating events that are likely to transpire can also produce emotional responses. Viewers who are able to infer what will soon happen may feel fear, anxiety, depression, joy, or amusement just thinking about what they expect. They may start to laugh, even though television characters are serious, because they infer that Gidget's pajama legs will soon drop down from under her coat much to everyone's exaggerated embarrassment. Again, the exact feeling, if any, that viewers experience will be jointly determined by what they expect will happen and by their liking and respect for the character(s) to whom it will happen.

Liking and admiration for characters are themselves constructed responses, evaluative outcomes that may occur during the process of making sense of television content. The culture in which one resides establishes a moral code and a set of criteria for evaluating actions not specifically sanctioned or interdicted by the moral code. Children use whatever they know about the code and criteria to evaluate characters, their motives, and their actions. In my own research, for instance, kindergartners disapproved of every television character they had seen engage in violence, whether the character was a "good guy" or a "bad guy," apparently because they believed aggression was always wrong and anyone who used it was therefore also wrong (Leifer & Roberts, 1972). Older children considered both aggressive actions and reasons for these actions in arriving at their evaluations of the same characters.

The amount of mental activity involved in arriving at these positive and negative evaluations varies according to the television content. Some motives and actions need only be recognized to be judged good or bad and reacted to accordingly. Others need to be considered in the context of earlier events, current actions of various characters, characters' personalities, abilities, and motives, and likely outcomes. Judgments about a character, and the resulting feelings for him or her, ordinarily require some mental effort to balance out the character's personality and abilities, the circumstances he or she faces, and the methods he or she uses to cope with these circumstances. The 90-pound weakling who goes to the aid of a damsel in distress should be judged rather differently than the behemoth who also goes to help her, and the subsequent feelings for the two characters should also be different.

As noted earlier, making sense of television content can include attributing motives to those who produced and broadcast that content. The attributed motives can then engender more general, diffuse positive or negative feelings toward the content. Around the age of seven, eight, or nine when children understand that commercials are intended to persuade them to like and want a product or service, they often feel very negatively toward commercials. They complain when they come on, criticize them, deny their claims, look away or talk, or leave the room. When evaluative activities are triggered by recognizing that an advertisement has come on, they then influence information processing and interpretation of the commercial content. Attributing less self-interested motives to those responsible for television content, motives such as informing, teaching, or inspiring, can lead in an analogous way to more positive evaluations.

Most evaluative activities depend to a greater or lesser degree on information-processing and interpretive activities. All require enough information processing to recognize the content being presented, and most require interpretive activities as well. Information must usually be integrated over time or across stimuli in one scene. Motives and feelings must usually be attributed to characters. Omitted events must be inferred, and forthcoming events, anticipated. Without activities such as these, emotions and reactions would rarely occur during television viewing.

Conversely, however, emotions and reactions, the evaluative side of things, influence information-processing and interpretive activities. Sometimes the influence is in the quality of the information processing and interpretation. When evaluative activities produce moderate amounts of arousal, mental activity is improved. Children pay more attention to content, process it better, and remember it better. Information processing and interpretation are less good when arousal is very low because children fail to invest enough energy in making sense of television content and when it is very high because they are distracted by whatever aroused them.

Another influence of emotions and reactions is on the content that is processed or interpreted. When a child has dysphoric, or bad, feelings during viewing, whether these feelings have been aroused by the television content or by some other event, the child is more likely to understand and remember negative content. Conversely, when the child has euphoric, or good, feelings during viewing, positive events are more likely to be understood and recalled. Perhaps this occurs because the child directs information processing and interpretation so as to maintain positive or negative feelings. Alternatively, the child's feelings may make more available to him or her some world knowledge and processing abilities that help construct meaning for content with a similar feeling tone.

Even after television viewing is all over, feelings can influence the apparent outcomes of other constructive activities during viewing. When a child feels badly, for instance, he or she is better able to recall the negatively toned aspects of a television program or those aspects viewed while feeling dysphoric. Conversely, when a child feels euphoric, he or she recalls more positively toned content or content viewed while feeling good. Testing children when they are both euphoric and dysphoric indicates that both positive and negative television content is stored in memory but that the content recalled tends to be of the same emotional tone as the child's feelings during recall. Once again, then, and in several different ways we see that the constructive processes are intertwined and interdependent rather than independent and sequential.

MAKING BETTER SENSE

Hilde Himmelweit and Wilbur Schramm, two pioneers in the study of children's transactions with television, recognized that children had to be active participants in determining television's meaning in their lives. Each provided specific evidence to support this view, but neither could describe very fully how children went about using television. Today, thanks to research and theory in the fields of cognitive psychology, psycholinguistics, sociolinguistics, ethnomethodology, mass communications, and children and television, we can describe in some detail the constructive processes children need to use to make sense of television content. We can easily recognize that children must be active participants in their transactions with television if they are going to extract any meaning from auditory and visual stimuli presented to them.

Most of the time children construct meaning for television content without even thinking about it. They attend to television's stimuli, choosing among and acting upon them to extract concrete and literal meaning. They also integrate together pieces of content, infer suggested but not depicted events, and attribute feelings and motives to characters. And they have emotional reactions to what they see, experiencing different feelings and assigning moral value to characters, actions, and events. These several information-processing, interpretive, and evaluative activities are at once independent and interdependent, operating simultaneously and sequentially in an intertwined pattern that can be complex and challenging for even the most sophisticated and skilled viewer.

Knowing how much may be required to construct meaning for television content, we better appreciate the difficulties children may encounter when trying to make sense of what they view. Social scientists will make better sense of children's transactions with television if they take constructive processes quite seriously, recognizing the many ways in which children's sense making activities may diverge from their own. Television producers will help children to make better sense of their programs and commercials if they also take this perspective, producing programming that can be understood without more or different world knowledge or more or better constructive abilities than their intended audience has. Finally, within a limited range, children can learn to make better sense of television content if their caretakers teach the world knowledge and constructive processes that are within children's grasp developmentally and that will help them to understand television better.

3

INFLUENCES ON UNDERSTANDING

How television content is understood—or how well it is understood—varies according to similarities between viewers and content, viewer needs and interests, viewer age, and television content characteristics.

We will now explore major influences on children's understanding of television content, again taking a middle position between the extremes of constructed and delivered meaning. Television delivers the same stimuli to all child viewers, but these stimuli vary enormously in the ease with which children can construct meaning for them that approximates what producers had in mind. Any meaning found for any television content was constructed independently by each child for himself or herself. However, because many children share similar knowledge of the physical, social, and spiritual world and of how to go about making sense of experience, large numbers of them may construct similar messages for the same set of television stimuli. When their knowledge differs, however, different children may reasonably be expected to construct different messages for the same content.

The major factors predicting differences in children's understanding of and reactions to television content can be roughly divided into similarity between viewers and content, viewer needs and interests, viewer age, and television content itself. In reviewing these factors, there will be more describing of the differences they produce than theorizing about how they work, because that best reflects the state of our knowledge. Also in line with research in the field, much of the chapter will be devoted to age differences in understanding television.

SIMILARITY BETWEEN VIEWERS AND CONTENT

In the last 30 years there have been recurring demonstrations that children are more likely to attend to, like, understand, and remember content that is conveyed by characters who in one way or another are similar to them. Elementary school students who viewed multicultural programs produced under the Emergency School Aid Act more often looked at and liked characters who shared their ethnic background (Nelson & Napior, 1976). Among seven-year-olds, a program featuring a family of the same social class was better understood than a program featuring a family of a different social class (Newcomb & Collins, 1979). Preteens and young teenagers better remembered content involving familiar characters and settings (Holaday & Stoddard, 1933). Seventh graders better remembered actions of characters of a similar social class and of characters of the social class the teenagers intended to join as adults (Maccoby & Wilson, 1957). These are but a sample of many studies showing that similarity influences children's understanding of television. They illustrate, too, that similarity can be achieved in several different ways: immutable personal characteristics (sex or ethnicity), mutable personal characteristics (social class or interests), and even aspirations (the child's) and "reality" (the character's).

What these findings do not show, but what should be remembered, is that similarity and dissimilarity do not operate willy-nilly to produce differences in children's responses to television. Children are sensitive to content structure and quality. They will rightly first attend to, like, understand, and remember main characters, central events or messages, and higher quality material. Having put first things first, they will operate on the basis of similarity when it involves a choice among main characters, major messages, or good content.

We know only a little about how similarity operates to produce differences in children's interactions with television. That children look more at similar characters (when they are equally important and on screen about the same amount of time) suggests that similarity influences the distribution of attention and effort during information processing of television stimuli. That children like similar characters more and learn more from them suggests that similarity increases arousal during viewing, which in moderate amounts would heighten attention and effort during viewing and lead to more learning. That children better understand content featuring families of similar social class and remember more from similar characters suggests that similarity allows children to draw upon their own background knowledge to help interpret and evaluate television content. Even without understanding precisely how similarity works, however, it is useful to know that it is one fairly reliable predictor of differences in children's understanding of television.

VIEWER NEEDS AND INTERESTS

A second predictor of differences in understanding television is the needs and interests children bring with them to the viewing experience. Children who regard television as an informative medium are more likely to invest in making sense of its content than are children who think of it only as a diverting or relaxing medium. Children who are interested in particular content for whatever reason (e.g., to talk with friends about or to parody) are also likely to give more effort to viewing. Finally, children who come to viewing free from pressing needs that can only be satisfied by something other than television are more likely to keep their attention on the the set and, hence, to understand its content.

Needs and interests operate to guide children's viewing, understanding, and recall so as to enhance the personal relevance of television content without distorting its reality. They do not lead children to dismiss important content irrelevant to their needs and interests. Nor do they lead children to ignore central content in favor of incidental content that better addresses their needs and interests. Nor do they lead children to watch much uninspiring, dull, or low quality content. Rather, like similarity, they operate more at the margins, guiding choices that can be made without sacrificing viewing pleasure or understanding of the main points of a program or commercial.

In communication research, "uses and gratifications" is the label applied to examination of the role of needs and interests in the transactions between children and television. As developed by the communications scholars, Jay Blumler and Elihu Katz (1974), the approach assumes that children have needs and seek gratifications, that they have experienced certain gratifications from their use of media, that they can and do choose to use media so as to obtain gratifications, and that they can reliably report on the gratifications obtained from their use of media. Since the original formulation, research has mostly focused on the uses and gratifications associated with different media, sometimes on those associated with different types of content within a medium, and only occasionally on those predicting understanding or recall.

Uses and gratifications research that includes children and television has provided some support for the validity and utility of the approach. Children seem to obtain somewhat different gratifications from using different media; they often use television for both entertainment and information gratifications; and they differentiate programs somewhat on the basis of the gratifications provided (see Brown, 1976; v. Feilitzen, 1976; Rubin, 1979; and Rubin & Rubin, 1982, for recent research and summaries), but few simple, definitive relationships have been found.

Only a few studies have explored links between children's uses of television and their learning from it, but those that have suggest that children's needs and interests partially predict what they take away from viewing. The effects of a mass media campaign to convey family planning information to teenagers were best understood, for instance, when the teenagers' needs for and interests in such information were also taken into account (Kline, Miller, & Morrison, 1974). Children's needs and interests, then, may operate to influence what effects television content has on them, as well as how much television is viewed, what content is watched, and what sense is made of it.

VIEWER AGE

A number of age-related differences in children's understanding of television have come to light in the past quarter century. When television first became popular, we often turned to basic research in child development, psychology, education, and sociology for help in predicting what it would mean to children of different ages. We still sometimes turn to these other fields for ideas and inspiration, but we also have developed our own body of research focusing specifically on children and television. It is this research, and it alone, that will be reviewed here.

The organization of this section will reflect the structure of the field, as it begins with the construction of meaning, continues with understanding of form and commercials, and ends with understanding of production and broadcasting. For each topic we want to convey a sense of why social scientists consider it important, what variables they have studied, and what age-related changes they have found. These changes will usually be described as general developmental trends, but a few specific age norms or markers will be offered to help pin down the trends.

Constructing Meaning for Content

In describing how people construct meaning for television content, three types of activities—information processing, interpretation, and evaluation—were identified. These types provide a convenient means for organizing our discussion of developmental changes in the ways in which children make sense of television. There is much to discuss, as the topic has been a focus of research in the last decade (see Collins, 1982, 1983; Dorr, 1980; Noble, 1975; and Rydin, 1983, for recent reviews).

One marked developmental pattern in the outcomes of information processing of television content is an increase throughout childhood and adolescence in the amount of information acquired. This was demonstrated as early as the 1930s in a benchmark study of information acquisition from entertainment films (Holaday & Stoddard, 1933). First, adults watched each film and wrote down every idea presented in it, including ideas that are factually incorrect in the real world. The total number of ideas they found was used as the standard. Children recalled less than half and adolescents no more than about three-quarters of all these ideas. At all ages, viewers recalled both factually correct and factually incorrect ideas, but the proportion of factually incorrect ideas decreased with increasing age.

More recently several researchers have demonstrated age-related increases in children's recall of important television content, including plot events, advertising claims, instructional content, news items, and principal messages in children's programming. Although exact figures vary by content and testing method, a rough representation of age-related changes in the learning of important content would be Leifer and Roberts' (1972) findings for understanding the motivations and consequences for important aggressive acts in entertainment programs: 5-year-olds correctly answered about 33% of the multiple-choice questions, 8-year-olds about 50%, 11-year-olds about 75%, and 18-year-olds about 95%.

A somewhat different developmental pattern obtains for recall of incidental rather than central information. Incidental information is all that content adults believe is unnecessary for understanding the plot of narrative programs, for knowing the main points of news, public affairs, and instructional content, or for grasping the claims of commercials. From preschool age to the end of childhood, there is a steady increase in recall of such incidental information, but from pubescence on there is a steady decrease in recall. Thus, there is an inverted U-shaped pattern for developmental changes in recall of incidental information, while the pattern for recall of central content is one of continued improvement.

Factors that surely contribute to developmental changes in children's recall of television content are changes in their abilities to attend to television stimuli, to select relevant stimuli, and to encode them properly. With development, children's patterns of attention to the television screen become more in tune with the information-processing demands of the content being broadcast. They take longer looks at slower paced narrative material and shorter looks at faster paced and/or segmented material. They look longer and more often at the television screen, look away more when content is unimportant than important, and look more often and longer at the important parts of each visual image. They more often select central rather than incidental content to encode. All these changes reflect increasing ability to attend to, select, and encode television content so that more of it and more of what is important will be remembered.

Another important factor influencing recall is age-related changes in children's internal models, or schemas, for the structure of television genres and for any content. The selection, encoding, and recall of information is to some extent organized by such schemas. Having a schema promotes learning, and having a better schema promotes better learning. Young children who do not know much about the structure of commercials have been found, for example, to increase their recall of commercial content after training about the types of information commercials usually contain. Analogously, developmental increases in children's recall of central content should be partially explained by increases with age in the accuracy of their schemas or scripts for different types of activities or events.

Children's schemas for plots improve with age. Young children have very simple schemas, usually involving little more than an initiating event, an attempt at a resolution, and the consequences of that resolution. Motives, plans, feelings, context, orientation, history, and nature of participants are infrequently part of the narrative models of children eight and younger. With increasing age, however, more elements (especially motives and feelings) are added to children's schemas for a plot and there is more expectation that plot elements should be related one to the other. These improved schemas for narrative structure should help children select and recall more altogether and more that is important to the plot.

Just as developmental changes have been found in children's information-processing activities, so have age-related differences been found in their interpretive activities. In terms of attributions, children have been shown to change in their inclination to attribute motives and feelings to television characters and in their ability to make accurate attributions. In retelling plots, for instance, nearly all children younger than about 10 omitted any mention of motives even though they were recounting a carefully edited 11-minute program right after seeing it (Collins, Berndt, & Hess, 1974). In the same study, about half of the 10-year-olds and two-thirds of the 13-year-olds included motives. Other studies have tested children's recognition of characters' motives or feelings and found substantial improvement up to about age 10. Even after this age, there are increases in children's abilities to attribute complex, competing, or subtle emotions to characters (see Dorr, Doubleday, & Kovaric, 1983, for a review).

Just as children change in their inclination and ability to attribute unseen emotions and motives to characters, so too do they change in inferring implied but not depicted events. Children younger than about 8 or 9 rarely infer missing content, and when they do their inferences are often incorrect. These children typically understand less of the explicit content and have less of the background knowledge needed to make correct inferences. Andrew Collins, the major contributor to research knowledge about information-processing and interpretive activities with television content, reports, however, that in his studies children younger than about 8 performed at chance level *even when* they knew every piece of explicit content needed for making correct inferences (Collins, 1982). This suggests young children have problems with the inference process itself, as well as lacking requisite knowledge of explicit television content and of relevant real-world activities. Further disrupting children's inferences is their over-reliance on stereotyped expectations about plot structure, even for plots that are not stereotypical. Inferences about television content have rarely been studied in adolescents, but at least up to age 13 we know there is a steady increase in children's inclination and ability to infer implied content.

Integration of content in different parts of a commercial or program also increases with age. Throughout childhood there is a steady improvement in sequencing the main events of a program correctly and a steady increase in the number of events that can be sequenced. Preschoolers tend to ignore plot or content continuity and to focus instead on isolated, interesting events in their recollection of television content. By about age 7 children prefer plotted programs to segmented, magazine-style programs and continuity to discontinuity. As we noted earlier, they have developed a rudimentary model for plots that apparently helps them encode, integrate, and recall television content. Even 7- or 8-year-olds, however, find integration of the elements of standard prime-time programs challenging, and their performance can be notably diminished by placing irrelevant content (e.g., commercials) between the central elements of a plot.

There is one last set of constructive activities with enough research evidence to warrant inclusion in this section. It is children's understandings of the reality, realism, purpose, credibility, truthfulness, or accuracy of television content. These are part of evaluation processes when children are constructing meaning for television content. One prominent focus of research in this area has been the realism of program content. Two others that will be covered later are the purpose, and hence credibility, truthfulness, and accuracy, of commercial advertising and the reality and purpose of entertainment programs.

There are marked changes throughout childhood in children's ideas about the reality of television program content. Preschoolers tend to think of it as completely real, because everything looks so lifelike—even if smaller and confined to the set. At some point, though, most realize that animated and puppet programs are not real. By about age 7 or 8 most know that even programs featuring real people are not necessarily glimpses of real life. They recognize news, commercials, cartoons, entertainment programs, and educational programs as different forms whose content has different ostensible reality values. Probably the most important learning about television program content reality has taken place by this age. Two things happen after that. For content that purports to represent the real world truthfully (e.g., news and public affairs), there is increasing appreciation for the ways in which it may be unreal, inaccurate, biased, misleading, or false; while for content that makes no such claims for itself, there is increasing appreciation for the ways in which it can be realistic. Both these refinements in understanding can continue to develop into adulthood.

These, then, are several ways in which children of different ages have been found to construct meaning for television content. A major shift in their transactions with television seems to occur sometime between the ages of 6 and 9, and a smaller shift probably occurs around adolescence. Whether one thinks of developmental change as stepwise or continuous, what is important is the fact of change. Children of different ages are likely to construct different meanings for what they view and to take different messages away from their viewing.

Understanding Form

The television messages children come to understand are primarily conveyed by characters' words and deeds and by settings and props, but they are also conveyed by the production techniques associated with them. Different camera angles suggest differences in power, point of view, and mood. The pace and style of editing are related to mood, implied power, and changes in place, time, or perspective. Music, laugh tracks, and special sound effects suggest mood and foreshadow or recall events. Special effects, such as slow motion, fades, and zooms, heighten a mood, suggest superhuman powers, and convey altered mental states. All such production techniques are often lumped together under the term television "form" to differentiate them from television "content."

Most social scientists and television producers assume that ordinary television viewing involves attending to and using both form and content cues to construct meaning for what is being watched. They also assume that content plays a much more important role than does form in conveying meaning, and it is for this reason that we have usually referred to television messages as television content in this book. This practice should not obscure the fact that messages are conveyed by both form and content. The research just reviewed assumed this and so says something about age-related differences in children's understanding of both form and content. Quite recently, though, a body of research has been developing that examines children's understanding of television form independent of television content (see Huston & Wright, 1983; Krull, 1983; Rice, Huston, & Wright, 1982; Salomon, 1979; and Watt & Welch, 1983, for examples).

The little evidence we now have suggests that analysis of form is rarely a very conscious activity of viewers, that it is ordinarily secondary to the analysis of content, and that understanding of it improves during childhood. More than one researcher has found child viewers, left to their own devices, to be insensitive to variations in form apart from those tied to variations in content and unlikely to analyze programming at the level of form. These tendencies change little with development. When form cues are connected with content cues and content is like children's experiences in everyday life, even very young children can properly interpret such form-content cues as change in perspective and change in place. When content cues are absent but multiple form cues are combined to convey particular messages (e.g., this content is for boys and this for girls) and children are directed to attend to form cues, even 6-year-olds can reliably interpret the meaning of at least some form cues. However, the ability to interpret such cues increases substantially at least up until adolescence.

Knowledge of the development of children's understanding of form, independent of content, is just now accumulating. Researchers are still struggling to conceptualize the complexities of the relationship between form and content in ordinary television and to develop assessment techniques that effectively separate form from content or, alternatively, pair one form with multiple, contrasting contents. As conceptualizations and assessment techniques become more sophisticated, we can expect a burst of knowledge about the development of understanding and use of form cues.

Understanding Commercials

Of all the television content children process, interpret, and evaluate, commercial advertising perhaps presents the most significant challenges. Educational, news, and public affairs programs intend to communicate certain factual, socially sanctioned content to children. Entertainment programs are designed to attract large viewing audiences without necessarily teaching or persuading them. Commercials, in contrast, are produced with the intention of persuading viewers to purchase (or have purchased for them) products and services, few of which in the case of children are essential to their well-being.

Usually products and services, packaging, advertising campaigns, and commercials are developed through a process of repeated field testing and revision. On average, the per-minute production costs for commercials are much higher than those for any other type of content, even prime-time entertainment programs. Because commercials have the goals they do, are for products and services designed to be attractive, and are produced with such a commitment to effectiveness, children need to be able to recognize them, understand their purpose, and identify their persuasive techniques so as to cope better with their messages (see Adler et al., 1980; Atkin, 1982; Ward, Wackman, & Wartella, 1977; and Wartella, 1980, for major reviews of work in this area).

By the time children are 6 to 8 years old they can more often than not differentiate commercials from programs. If they are asked to describe differences, the majority can volunteer one or more correct differences. If they are asked to raise their hands or shout out when a commercial appears during broadcasting, a majority can do so more often than not. At 8 they are still confused by public service announcements, those short commercial-like messages for dental health, cooperation, and the 4-H clubs, but otherwise children are usually accurate in identifying commercials when they appear during viewing. Identification is not, however, based on what adults regard as the most important attribute of commercials—their intent to persuade. Rather it is based on such concrete characteristics as length, humor, music, animation, and liveliness.

Understanding the persuasive intent of commercials comes somewhat later than does ability to recognize them, although recognition is certainly not a prerequisite for understanding persuasive intent. No matter how preschoolers are tested, the majority do not know that commercials are intended to persuade them to want goods and services. Somewhere between the ages of 7 and 9 the majority of children are likely to understand persuasive intent. Younger children in this age range do better when assessment involves simple multiple choice questions and photographs; older children can explain the purpose of commercials in their own words without any supporting materials. Either way, around the middle of childhood the majority of children understand that commercials are intended to persuade rather than inform or entertain (see Federal Trade Commission, 1981, for a thorough, policy-oriented review of age-related changes in understanding persuasive intent).

Having learned about persuasive intent, children can still learn much about how commercial content is organized to achieve its goal. It is not uncommon to find that children who have just become aware of persuasive intent are convinced all commercials are full of out and out lies. They sit around the set scornfully denying that a paper towel could absorb so much moisture or that a toy hot rod would really flip twice, right itself, and charge forward again. Gradually they learn that commercials may possess some truth and are limited by law in what they can do. Near adolescence, children have acquired some awareness of common persuasive techniques (e.g., testimonials from popular entertainers and appeals to social status needs) and how they are realized in commerical advertising. This understanding can help children evaluate advertising claims sensibly and gain more control over the type and amount of influence commercials exert on them.

Understanding Production and Broadcasting

Understanding how television content is created can help children evaluate the reality and credibility of what they see. Children who understand production processes may not be so influenced by the apparent reality of what they see. They know television content is an illusion created by clever production techniques and so evaluate it on criteria other than appearance. Children who do not know about television production processes do not have so ready a reason to reject the apparent reality of what they see and are more inclined to feel it must be real.

Similarly, children who do not know about the structure and major goals of the instructional, public, and commercial broadcasting systems are at a disadvantage. Children who can accurately supply motives for the creation and distribution of content on each system (respectively to educate, to inform and enlighten, and to make money) can use these attributions to adjust their views of the credibility of content on each system. Children who cannot make such attributions have one less criterion to use in assessing the reality or realism of what they are watching.

Throughout childhood there is very clear development in understanding how television content is created (see Dorr, 1983). Many very young viewers believe that there are little people inside the set, that a television character can actually see them, or that events occurring on the screen are going on exactly that way in real life. When he was three, my older son said "Mommy, look at this. Mommy! Mommy, look!" to a live television interview of me that his father was watching. My son walked away in disgust when I failed to respond to him.

Robert Hawkins (1977) has coined the phrase "Magic Window Reality" to describe this period when children seem to believe there is a literal reality to what they are watching on television. As children mature, they move away from this belief, learning more about the ways in which television content is constructed. In one study, for instance, 58% of 5- and 6-year-olds did not understand that television characters were portrayed by actors; 29% of 8-year-olds also did not understand, but 45% completely understood and 26% partially understood; and among 11- and 12-year-olds, 65% completely understood (Fernie, 1981). Like this study, other research suggests that by about the age of 8 most children know television content is usually created rather than captured and understand the basics of the production process.

Although they know the basics, most 8-year-olds do not have a sophisticated understanding of the production process nor do they always use their understanding appropriately. Many do not know enough about production techniques to explain away such content as superhuman strength, superimposition of characters on unlikely backgrounds, or operating space vehicles. Many adolescents, too, can be uncertain about aspects of television production, for instance, not recognizing the potential biases in production choices of camera shots and news items.

Even knowledgeable children and adolescents can incorporate their correct understandings into wrong conclusions. A student of mine once interviewed a teenager who knew that prime-time programs were scripted and acted but also believed that lawyer Perry Mason always won on television because he selected only his successful cases to be written up for production. At seven, my older son decided that producers used make-up to make aged actors look young before they were actually shot to death in crime dramas. Thus, there is considerable development through adolescence in understanding the production process and putting this understanding to work in evaluating the reality of content.

Understanding of the broadcast industry develops later, more slowly, and less completely than does understanding of television production techniques (see Dorr, 1983). It is not until mid-adolescence that children understand any of the economic motivations guiding commercial broadcasting. Even at this age, and on into late adolescence, the most frequently voiced "knowledge" about broadcasting was classified in my work as misconceptions or isolated facts rather than as correct understanding of the commercial broadcasting system. Only in adulthood do a majority of people understand the interactions among ratings, advertising, and income. Older children and adolescents probably understand the public and instructional broadcasting systems to be something different from the commercial broadcasting system, but the revenue structure, organization, and regulation of broadcasting are not that well known even among adults.

Research on persuasion and attitude change suggests that people are not so quick to accept messages delivered by less credible communicators. Applying this idea to television, it seems desirable that child viewers understand how much television content is constructed and how often its primary goal is to deliver audiences to advertisers. If children chose to apply such knowledge to their reasoning about television content, they might better evaluate its reality, realism, and truthfulness. By about 8 years of age children apparently know how television content can be and usually is created, but it is not until adolescence that they have any appreciation for the strong financial motives guiding so many production and broadcasting decisions. Thus, throughout development children always know less than they could to assess television's credibility as a communicator, but by about age 8 and again by mid-adolescence they have acquired important knowledge to help in this evaluation activity.

TELEVISION CONTENT

Discussion thus far has focused entirely on children, but it is now time to turn to the other participant in the transaction between children and television to examine how differences in television content also predict differences in understanding. We have frequently noted that television content varies in the challenges it presents to children who want to make sense of it, just as children vary in how they make sense of content. Having so far given a lot of attention to children, we want to turn the table to illustrate how television content characteristics can influence understanding and to describe effective procedures for producing understandable content.

Content Characteristics

Many content characteristics that influence children's understanding are just the flip side of what has already been presented for children. To describe them one need only do some rephrasing; for instance, more understandable content for young children features children, clearly depicts all major messages, does not require much inference, and presents items of central content without intervening irrelevant content. Rather than rephrasing everything that has already been said, here we will simply provide a few illustrations of the importance of content characteristics for children's understanding of television.

A recent study nicely demonstrates the effects of program pace, continuity, and format on children's understanding (Wright et al., 1984). For this study 16 children's programs from both commercial and public channels were selected and edited so as to be divided evenly into categories: well-structured narrative plot versus magazine style, high versus low pace, and animation versus live action. After viewing, children were asked to put in order five photographs of important scenes in each program and then five photographs from within one segment (magazines) or one scene (narratives). Both 5- to 6-year-olds and 8- to 9-year-olds did better for plotted than for magazine-style programs and for low- than for high-paced programs. Whether a program was animated or live action did not matter for sequencing photographs from the whole program. For sequencing within a segment or scene, children did better on live than animated programs except with high paced magazine-style programs, which were sequenced better when they were animated rather than live action. And, yes, child variables mattered too: Older children generally sequenced photographs better than younger children. This study, then, nicely illustrates how variations in television programs—and variations in viewers—act to produce variations in children's understanding of program content.

Similar kinds of findings have been reported in studies of commercial advertising. One study, for example, demonstrated that very few children understood the meaning of the then standard disclaimer "Assembly required" while most understood an alternative like "You have to put it together" (Liebert, Sprafkin, Liebert, & Rubinstein, 1977). Another demonstrated that the now standard separator between children's programs and commercials, which features animated program characters and a voiceover saying "Program X will be right back after these messages," does not in any way help young children to identify the ensuing commercials (Palmer & McDowell, 1979). An alternative separator in which the visual was a red stop sign and the voiceover said "OK, kids, get ready, here comes a commercial" dramatically increased commercial recognition by 4-, 6-, and 8-year-old boys (Ballard-Campbell, 1983). All three studies show that variations in commercial content influence children's understanding and suggest what more intelligible commercial messages might look like.

It has always been tempting for children's advocates to assume there are simple formulas for producing understandable children's programs and commercials. Some want to outlaw animation, because they believe it leads to banal, easily understood programs with very little plot. Others advocate lively magazine-style programs for very young children, because they believe the style holds attention better, requires less integration, and leads to better understanding of messages. Still others believe children cannot understand crime dramas or situation comedies, because the plots are complicated, the programs require much inference and integration, and the ideas are mature. If these beliefs were correct and formulas based on them worked, then it would be easy to develop hard and fast guidelines for production companies, broadcasters, and regulators. No wonder it is tempting to look for simple answers.

Unfortunately, research does not consistently support very many simple formulas. Wright and associates' (1984) study clearly showed that animation need not lead any more than does live action to banal, easily understood, or unplotted programs and called into question the common assumption that preschoolers are best served by fast-paced, magazine-style programs. Other work has clearly shown that prime-time westerns, prime-time crime dramas, and Saturday morning children's programs can vary more within than across program type in how understandable they are to children as young as 4 and as old as 18 (Leifer & Roberts, 1972). It is not simple formulas alone, then, that will lead to more understandable television content for children. They may help a production get started, but what is ultimately needed is careful attention to the details of language, visualization, audiovisual coordination, plot, continuity, sequencing, pace, characters, and characterization. Only a coordinated, thoughtful use of all elements of a production will lead to content that viewers will easily understand as producers intended.

Production Processes

The production process is complex (see Cantor, 1980, and Crane, 1980, for descriptions) and even program creators with the best of intentions can run into problems (see Elliott, 1972, for an illuminating case study), but those who have produced the best content for children have developed several strategies for increasing their success to failure ratios. First, and probably most important, is hiring a staff with ideas, creativity, good values, understanding of children, and the desire to communicate effectively with them (see Siegel, 1980, for a critique of commercial broadcasting on these grounds). Second is providing for input from experts in the content area, in instructional methods, in children's transactions with television, in persuasion, in humor, and the like (see Meyer, 1983, for examples). Such experts provide helpful information before production begins and useful feedback on such preliminary products as outlines, scripts, storyboards, and rough cuts.

The third strategy, and perhaps the sine qua non of the more successful production groups, is conducting what has come to be known as formative research (see Lesser, 1974; Mielke, 1983; Palmer, 1983; and Rockman, 1983, for descriptions). The issues addressed in formative research are those most crucial to the success of the endeavor: Do children like the content? Do they attend to the content? Do they understand the intended messages? Do they construct unintended messages from the content? Are these unintended messages desirable or undesirable? Do they find the content credible? How can the content be changed to better reach its goals?

The questions of formative research are completely practical, tied exclusively to particular television content and its intended audience. Formative research is neither theoretical in its questions nor ideal in its methods (see Burdach, 1983, for discussion), but it invariably improves the television content created for children. When formative research is combined with a highly skilled staff and appropriate expert advice, the television content that is created will be attractive and understandable to children. It may not be a million-dollar winner, but it will always be better than it would otherwise have been.

VIVE LA DIFFERENCE

Television is a mass medium, but it does not and should not operate as though the masses are all the same when it comes to television viewing. The individuals who make up the masses pick what to watch, construct meaning for it, and place value on it to some extent according to what they are like, what they are interested in, what values they hold, what they already know, and what information-processing, interpretive, and evaluative abilities they have. They are more likely to tune in, attend to, like, understand, and remember programs and ads that feature sympathetic characters similar to them in age, sex, race, ethnicity, social class, religion, life circumstances, or any other quality that figures importantly in their self-definition. Likewise, they will opt for, understand, and value programming that addresses their particular needs and interests.

To be successful, then, in attracting and communicating to an audience, television producers and broadcasters must understand the different segments of the American public and take them into account. If they want to draw any particular segment into their audience, then they must program for it. To attract girls, for instance, they need to produce high quality material that casts females in some lead roles and makes them important to a story or topic that is itself interesting to girls (e.g., interpersonal relationships rather than aggressive adventures). In the 1970s a major network and the business school of a prestigious university each suggested the network use these principles to appeal to the rising black middle class, thereby increasing the network's viewing audience, its ratings, and its profits. Some Hispanics today urge that producers, advertisers, and broadcasters can reap similar rewards if they provide more material that features and appeals to the increasing numbers of Hispanics in the United States.

For those interested in children's transactions with television, age-related differences in how they make sense of and use television content are extraordinarily important. The research literature unequivocally demonstrates such differences in virtually every area studied. All scholarly work should take age into account. Those who want to use television deliberately to convey messages to children must also know about developmental changes in information processing, interpretation, and evaluation of programming and advertising content. Content is not equally appropriate for children of all ages; the changes from infancy through adolescence in interests, knowledge of the physical and social world, and ability to construct meaning for content are too great not to attend to them.

The challenge faced by instructional, public, and commercial broadcasting alike is that of finding the right level of segmentation for their audiences. Television production is too expensive to gear it to individuals or even small groups, but broadcasters who completely ignore the diversity of the American public will by and large fail in their mission to instruct, enlighten, inform, entertain, and generally serve the public interest, convenience, and necessity. Broadcasters may never be so enthusiastic about the heterogeneity of the American public as to shout, "Vive la différence!" but those who want to do a good job will learn about and take into account the important differences among those already in their audience and those who could join their audience if only the right content were provided.

4

EFFECTS OF TELEVISION CONTENT

Many people believe that television, like other popular media, can have both beneficial and harmful effects on children. Research confirms that its messages can at least sometimes affect the information, attitudes, and behaviors of youth today.

Television can play four roles in children's lives. One is that of a time-consuming activity—a relaxing reward after work is done or an absorbing distraction taking time away from homework, household chores, and outside play. A second is that of a social (or nonsocial) event—an opportunity to snuggle with parents or to escape from quarrelsome siblings. A third is that of an information-processing task—a medium that requires looking and listening simultaneously and remembering a chain of events whose continuity may be interrupted by irrelevant content. A fourth and final role is that of an information-providing experience—a source of knowledge or prejudice, a teacher of what to buy and how to play, fight, and love.

Most research has focused on television as a provider of "information" that may affect children's ideas, information, feelings, beliefs, attitudes, and behaviors. Some television content is created primarily to inform, educate, or persuade children. Researchers have asked whether, how much, how well, and why it succeeds. Most television content is created primarily to entertain. Researchers have nonetheless asked if this fare does not also inform, educate, or persuade children. Here we will examine how researchers have gone about this work and what they have learned. In later chapters we will explore arguments engendered by their findings about television's role as an information provider and will learn more about television's other three roles as a time-consuming activity, a social event, and an information-processing task.

MEDIA EFFECTS THROUGH HISTORY

Throughout recorded history children have had opportunities to participate in some experiences similar to those they have with television today. Borrowing from the sociologist Erving Goffman, we will call them "framed experiences." In his influential book *Frame Analysis* (1974), Goffman suggested that some experiences (e.g., rituals, games, theater) select a part of life and bring it into high relief, much like a framed painting on the wall. What is selected from life takes on special importance. Its elements are organized so that participants encounter orderliness, sequence, and apparent causation. The frames help organize and make sensible everyday experiences that are in reality disorderly and fluid. Goffman's analysis included many types of experiences, but we will focus on just a few.

Like paintings, what we have called framed experiences are there for children to consume but not to join as ordinary social interaction. There are literal or figurative brackets around them. Books, films, radio, newspapers, magazines, computers, and television all present framed experiences in which children cannot directly participate. Live events such as troubador songs, minstrel shows, poetry readings, plays, operas, oral stories, street theater, and puppet shows also present framed experiences, but children can join in them if they choose to. They know not to. Their role is that of audience member, consumer of a live framed experience that is selected, organized, and presented in such a way as to emphasize and clarify a slice of life.

Historical Examples

The Greek philosopher Plato, living 400 years before Christ, recognized the potential of framed experiences to influence youth. In *The Republic*, Plato's blueprint for an ideal State in which justice, truth, and wisdom prevail, he explained some special needs and vulnerabilities of children:

> You know also that the beginning is the most important part of any work, especially in the case of a young and tender thing; for that is the time at which the character is being formed and the desired impression is more readily taken. (Book II, pp. 320-321)
>
> For a young person cannot judge what is allegorical and what is literal; anything that he receives into his mind at that age is likely to become indelible and unalterable; and therefore it is most important that the tales which the young first hear should be models of virtuous thoughts. (Book II, p. 321)
>
> For if . . . our youth seriously listen to such unworthy representations of the gods, instead of laughing at them as they ought, hardly will any

> of them deem that he himself, being but a man, can be dishonoured by similar actions; neither will he rebuke any inclination which may arise in his mind to say and do the like. (Book III, p. 326)

Plato believed that all framed experiences should be created and performed with the welfare of youth in mind. It is clear in *The Republic* that he included fact and fiction presented in drama, history, narration, poetry, music, and lyrics—every form of framed experience available at that time. He went to great lengths to be clear that they all mattered: "Whatever be the sort of poetry, epic, lyric or tragic, in which the representation is given" and whatever "the words, the melody, and the rhythm" of songs and odes they must all be attended to.

For every framed experience, Plato believed its content could be a crucial influence on youth. Negative influences should be avoided: The gods should not lie or deceive or rape; gods and historical figures should not lament, beg, weep, or wail; epic heroes should not be motivated by love of money; and no one—not even mortal men or demigods—should stoop to vile or debasing humor. Positive influences should be sought: Soldiers should obey their commanders; gods, epic heroes, and mortal men alike should exercise self-control in sensual pleasures; famous men should engage in deeds of endurance; and heroes should be sufficient unto themselves their own happiness and least in need of other men.

Even the style for conveying good content came under scrutiny in the ideal State, for Plato realized that the messages in framed experiences were conveyed by "both matter and manner." He advocated that the ideal State "employ for our souls' health the rougher and severer poet or storyteller, who will imitate the style of the virtuous only, and will follow those models which we prescribed at first" (Book III, p. 331) and that its musicians eschew harmonies expressive of sorrow ("mixed or tenor Lydian and the full-toned or bass Lydian") and of softness and drinking ("Ionian and Lydian"; Book III, p. 331). As in all his writings, Plato was thorough and consistent in his plans for using framed experiences to help develop the ideal citizens of the ideal State, and he was persuasive in his reasons for urging these plans.

Books, whether laboriously copied by hand as in Plato's time or quickly printed at a press, have always been treated as potentially influential framed experiences. The power of informative, educational, and persuasive tracts has always been recognized, as at many times has the potential of fiction. Catholic clergy once hesitated to translate the Bible into the vernacular for fear the laity would give more credence to what the Bible said than to how the clergy interpreted it. Libraries and schools today refuse to own certain novels or to loan them to children, because they fear the mature or un-American content of these fictional works will be an undesirable influence on children.

At one time even opera was recognized as a framed experience that could influence audience members. Today, most of us find opera so elitist, hard to understand, and irrelevant that we cannot imagine anyone would ever worry about the effects of an operatic work on its audience. But officials once worried. Verdi's opera *Rigoletto* was banned from Venice in 1850 until substantial changes were made in it. The Austrian military governor, again in power after the revolt of 1848, "naturally frowned upon anything that set the ruling caste in a bad light, and even an unsuccessful attempt at assassination was considered highly undesirable as putting ideas into hotheads" (Hussey, 1963, p. 68). Before the opera could be performed, therefore, the title was changed, the king became a minor duke, the worst offenses of the king-duke were exorcised, the assassination attempt was trivialized, and the Kingdom of France turned into the minor duchy of Mantua.

Interpreting the Historical Record

Some would say the historical record shows thoughtful people have always recognized that which researchers have recently confirmed: That those who create framed experiences select out of their culture what is important and organize it into meaningful patterns that enculturate children and influence adults. Others argue quite differently. They note that concern for epics, operas, comic books, films, and radio has come and gone, each in its own time, and suggest that ceasing to worry means there never was any reason to worry. According to this line of reasoning, officials' worries about *Rigoletto* were misguided in 1850 in Austria because similar worries are ridiculous in 1985 in the United States.

There is no way finally to resolve the disagreement, as research about the social effects of framed experiences only began in the twentieth century. However, Goffman's theory of framing, research on the effects of radio, films, books, and television, and the historical record all suggest that framed experiences have existed throughout history, that they can carry important social content, and that they can influence those who encounter them. Exactly what framed experience and what content are influential for which people change through history. Medieval morality plays once reached many people with their culturally important messages about how to live an upstanding life. Plays are not so important today, but their social functions may have been taken over by some television programs. Many believe they have, especially for children.

SOCIETY REACTS TO TELEVISION

At the advent of television, thoughtful parents and social commentators recognized it would be an important framed experience for children. They saw television captivating youngsters, bringing them a fabulously enlarged and lively window on the world. Some worried that this world would too often be an unsavory one; others worried television would seduce children away from desirable activities. Many, however, waxed enthusiastic about the opportunities television presented for showing children the wonders of the world and the goodness of humankind, bringing master teachers to all schools, and providing a happy time for the whole family to be together. Today most people believe that, all things considered, children are better off with television than without it, and some programs, series, specials, and channels are lauded for a job well done.

Parents and social critics are, however, also very much aware of television's faults. One observer argues that television introduces children to an adult world they should not yet know about and holds this "total disclosure medium" responsible for the disappearance of childhood (Postman, 1982). Others find it violent, sexist, racist, and commercial (Mankiewicz & Swerdlow, 1978). Another wants to abolish it altogether (Mander, 1978). Parents complain that content is too violent, sexy, or amoral, not uplifting enough, and too likely to give children a case of "the gimmes" (Bower, 1973; Yankelovich & White, 1977). Overall, children may be better off with television, but it is not an unmitigated boon to their lives.

S. I. Hayakawa, the semanticist, ex-President of San Francisco State University, and ex-Senator from California, has been especially colorful in his indictment of television. In one paper written during the heyday of student activism, Hayakawa (1968, p. 2) compared television to a sorcerer:

> Suppose . . . that your children . . . are snatched away from you for three or four or more hours a day by a powerful sorcerer. This sorcerer is a story-teller and a spinner of dreams. He plays enchanting

> music; he is an unfailingly entertaining companion. He makes the children laugh; he teaches them jingles to sign [sic]; he is constantly suggesting good things to eat and wonderful toys for their parents to buy them. . . . The sorcerer is always fascinating so that [children] sit there as if drugged, absorbing messages that parents did not originate and often do not even know about.

Hayakawa believed that the effects of this sorcerer on children were nothing short of disastrous. Faced with activism from students who also happened to be the first generation to grow up under the sorcerer's spell, Hayakawa (pp. 5-6) was specific in his condemnation:

> It is my impression that militant young people, far from being "disillusioned" with democratic processes, are totally unacquainted with them, since they are rarely shown on television. . . . If young people did not learn about the complexities of the democratic process from their years of viewing television, what did they learn? They learned that social problems are never complicated; they are simply the conflicts between the good guys and bad guys. Bad guys can never be reasoned with—you can only shoot it out with them. . . . Young people also learned from commercials that there is an instant, simple solution to all problems. . . . Television documentaries about the problems of the world offer neat, half-hour wrapups of compelx events. Highlights are selected, while boring, tedious details are left out. Time is compressed, cause and effect are simplified. In situation dramas, people are presented not in the full complexity of their humanity, like people in real life, but in stereotyped roles. They therefore arrive at their emotional responses quickly and easily. . . . In private as in public affairs, life is not too hard to understand. That's what television says.

Today there is a large body of research exploring television's role in children's lives (see Comstock, Chaffee, Katzman, McCombs, & Roberts, 1978, for review). It permits a scientific assessment of the validity of some of these claims for and against television, leading ultimately to a more balanced understanding of the medium's possibilities, achievements, and failures.

TYPES OF TELEVISION CONTENT EFFECTS RESEARCH

By now many hundreds of studies have explored the effects of television content on child viewers. The topics of study may be characterized by the content presented to children (e.g., mathematics, aggression, or sex roles) and by the type of effect expected from viewing the content (e.g., acquisition of knowledge or change in behavior). Methods of study may be characterized by the type of research design and by the extent to which the research materials and experiences are like those of everyday life.

Topics Studied

Virtually every imaginable type of content has been the subject of at least one study. This includes research using specific pieces of programming: the commercial series *Lassie* and its effects on children's helping behaviors (Sprafkin, Liebert, & Poulos, 1975); nutrition public service announcements and their effects on knowledge about snack foods, stated food preferences, and actual snack food choices (Peterson, Jeffrey, Bridgewater, & Dawson, 1984); and the Watergate hearings and their effects on children's images of and trust in government leaders (Hawkins Pingree, & Roberts, 1975). It also includes research about types of programming and extended viewing of programming: a heavy diet of commercial crime drama and action adventure series and its effects on aggressive behavior (Belson, 1978); an entire televised mathematics course and its effects on standardized math achievement (Almstead & Graf, 1960); and many hours of watching commerical television and the effects on attitudes about men's and women's characteristics and roles (Frueh & McGhee, 1975), on knowledge of entertainers (Schramm et al., 1961), and on desire for advertised products (Clancy-Hepburn, Hickey, & Neville, 1974).

In the past 30 years, effects in three content areas have been extensively explored. Beginning in the 1950s, there have been many studies of how well television can teach children traditional academic information and skills. Beginning in the 1960s, there have been even more studies of how much television influences children's aggressive behaviors and their attitudes toward and expectations for aggression. Finally, beginning in the 1970s, there have been many studies of how much television influences children's social attitudes, social cognitions, and positive social behaviors. Throughout these three decades, effects in other content areas, such as politics, government, commerical advertising, and popular culture, have also been investigated, but to a lesser extent.

Effects arising from viewing television content can be divided according to the domain influenced: information, attitudes, or behaviors. For research about television effects on citizenship, for example, studies would then be classified as studies of effects on knowledge about political processes and office holders, attitudes toward the United States and voting, and actual participation in governance or electoral activities. Most often in this scheme information is believed to influence attitudes and behaviors, and attitudes are believed to influence behaviors. Informational effects are easiest to obtain, attitudinal effects are harder, and behavioral effects are hardest.

An alternative scheme conceptualizes effects according to the internal process of influence: acquisition, enhancement, or change. It considers what a child already knows, believes, and/or does in the particular content area and what messages the televised content presents. If a child knows, believes, or does nothing in the content area, then for content effects to be demonstrated television's messages need only be acquired. If a child already knows, believes, or does something in the content area, then for television effects to be demonstrated the messages can either enhance what is already known, believed or done or—more difficult still—change what is already known, believed, or done.

Methods of Study

The effects of television content have been assessed using both experimental and nonexperimental designs. The experimental design, randomly assigning children to two or more groups having contrasting experiences (e.g., instructional programs about careers and neutral animal films), allows one to make relatively unambiguous inferences about the causes of any obtained differences between the two or more groups. If children who watch the career programs then have higher career aspirations than peers who watch the animal films and if children in the two groups were drawn from the same population and random assignment was properly done, it is pretty safe to assume the career programs produced higher career aspirations in children viewing them. Experimental designs are desirable, because—in social science parlance—they permit unambiguous causal inference; that is, they make it relatively safe to assert that any group differences that show up are caused by the experimentally manipulated differences in prior experience.

In nonexperimental designs children are not randomly assigned to the contrasting experiences they have. Instead the differing experiences occur because of the children's own interests or abilities, what their parents or teachers are like, where they live, or a host of other factors. A nonexperimental design in the effects of career programs might contrast children in one school district that chose to show the programs with children in another district that chose not to show them. If results indicated that children in the first district had higher career aspirations, it would be more difficult to attribute them to the television programs than it would with an experimental design. The district in which the career education programs were shown might (1) serve children who already have higher career aspirations because they come from families of higher socioeconomic status, or (2) have an active career education and counseling program, or (3) choose the programs as enrichment material because their students are especially interested in careers.

The strength of a nonexperimental design resides in the possibilities it provides for inferring "real world" effects. Because experimental designs require considerable control of children's experiences, it is often difficult to make them very realistic. With nonexperimental designs, in contrast, one can fairly easily study children who on their own in everyday life watch the television content being studied, who watch real programs or commercials conveying the content, who watch for days, months, or years on end, who watch in their own homes or schools, and who show (or do not show) television's effects as they would naturally occur in everyday life. Nonexperimental designs are desirable, because—again in social science jargon—they permit greater ecological validity; that is, they make it possible to choose realistic research conditions and measures, circumstances very much like those of everyday life.

When one is interested in the effects of television content, ecological validity is just as important as unambiguous causal inference. One wants to be sure that television viewing at home, an ordinary, unremarkable experience for children, operates in a similar fashion to television viewing in a laboratory or other experimental setting, an extraordinary experience for children. Similarly, one wants to be sure that the informational, attitudinal, or behavioral effects one is studying will show up in children's everyday interactions as well as in special measurement situations.

In studying children's real-life transactions with television content, varied research designs and methods are desirable. The experimental design provides the surest test of whether television's messages affect viewers. With appropriate controls, nonexperimental designs are also informative about the causes of effects, but there is always more room to question the role of television. More ecologically valid methods provide the greatest assurance that everyday experiences and everyday outcomes are being studied.

Less ecologically valid methods increase the likelihood that the events of interest will occur and be relatively unadulterated by other events, but they almost always fall short of fully representing everyday life as children live it. To learn the most, then, one looks for designs and methods that provide as much unambiguous causal inference and ecological validity as possible. In several content areas now there is a raft of studies that taken altogether meet these conditions and so permit us to say much about television as an information-providing experience.

Absence of a Constructivist Perspective

Despite this large literature, few studies exhibit any use of the constructivist perspective. Most employ samples of content that researchers believe represent messages in a particular area (e.g., aggression, geography, arithmetic, sex roles). This material is shown to children and their responses in the same area, again as defined by researchers, are measured. It is delivered meaning, as constructed by researchers, that is studied assuming it is similar to the meaning children themselves construct for the content. The meaning of the outcome measures is also defined by researchers not children. To the extent that researchers and children share a common culture and common means for making sense of experience, these research practices are defensible.

EFFECTS OF TELEVISION CONTENT

There is, by now, conclusive evidence that television content can affect children's information, attitudes, and behaviors and that its effects are generally not different from those of other influences in their lives. How large these effects are, how often they occur, for whom they occur, how long they last, and how significant they are for American society, are all unresolved questions about which there is vigorous debate (see Chapter 5). We will turn to the arguments after we get the basic facts straight for the two questions most often asked about television content effects.

The most frequent question is whether television content affects children at all. A large body of research provides a clear and consistent answer: It does. Children exposed to content over television more often than not know, believe, or do more in the content area than do children exposed to completely different content over television, children given other irrelevant experiences (e.g., conversation with the experimenter or toy play), children given no other contrasting experiences, or children with a lesser amount of exposure to the same televised content. The effects show up for every type of content that has been investigated (e.g., behaving aggressively, wanting advertised products, and knowing about foreign countries) and for every type of effect (i.e., information, attitude, behavior or acquire, enhance, change). The effect is usually clearer and stronger and the causal role of television is more nearly unambiguous in research employing experimental designs and less ecologically valid methods. However, research employing more ecologically valid methods in experimental and nonexperimental designs also generally supports this conclusion.

The second most frequent question is whether the effects of content conveyed by television are the same as the effects of the "same" content conveyed some other way. Children taught by television are contrasted with children taught the same content by parents, peers, teachers, films, books, or radio programs. The two groups of children are not consistently or significantly different. These findings are based primarily on research using experimental designs to study the effects of instructional programs. The few studies comparing the influence of television and other socializers on aggressive and prosocial behavior support these conclusions.

To state that answers to the two main questions about television content effects are clear and consistent is not to suggest that every study supports them. There are some very well-executed studies indicating that television content in a particular area has no effect, has effects only under very circumscribed conditions, or has effects different from those of other experiences with the same content. For instance, one experiment found that a prime-time crime drama program showing theft from a charity box had no effect on viewers' thefts from a similar box in a gift distribution center (Milgram & Shotland, 1973). It is important to recognize the existence and validity of such research, to uncover the reasons for the results, to weigh the findings in deciding whether and how television content affects children, and to decide how the disconfirming research establishes limiting conditions within which television may be effective.

Most demonstrated television content effects are of the following sort: Children exposed to content X show more of X in a postviewing measurement situation than do children exposed to no content X or less content X. Children who watch a CBS national citizenship test at home know more about American government officials and practices than do children of the same age, sex, ethnicity, and social class who do not watch it (Alper & Leidy, 1970). English-Canadian children who watch short segments portraying positive images of French-Canadian and nonwhite Canadian children have more positive attitudes toward these children than do their peers who do not watch such segments (Gorn, Goldberg, & Kanungo, 1976). And institutionalized children whose regular television diets are adjusted to include more prosocial content and less aggressive content become more positive in their social interactions with other children (Rubinstein & Sprafkin, 1982). In other words, what children see on television is what children take away from it for their own information, attitudes, and behaviors.

Very occasionally there are boomerang effects where children exposed to content X show more of not-X rather than X. For example, in an experiment by Pingree (1978), third-grade girls and boys and eighth-grade girls who saw ads featuring women in less traditional roles (e.g., a woman doctor talking about a Dupont product) endorsed more nontraditional roles for women than did their peers who saw more traditional women (e.g., a housewife explaining the advantages of Cheer to her daughter). Eighth-grade boys, however, became more traditional after seeing the nontraditional women. We can speculate that these boys were especially concerned with establishing their masculine identities and that the nontraditional ads reminded them it is more difficult to do this when men's and women's roles overlap. Whatever the explanation, the results are an interesting illustration of a boomerang effect.

Boomerang effects do not occur often enough, however, to provide support for the once popular notion that watching television could be a cathartic experience. Catharsis is a concept at least as old as Greek drama. It is said to occur when a particular feeling upon which one might act is drained away in a vicarious experience involving that emotion. Accordingly, viewing a play in which Oedipus experiences and acts upon anger with his father and love for his mother permits audience members, especially men, to release hostility for their fathers and affection for their mothers without experiencing any negative consequences that might occur should they give vent to these feelings in everyday interactions with their parents. There is little evidence that catharsis ordinarily occurs while watching television, no matter how much emotion viewers feel at the time. Instead, most often television content has no effects or produces effects in the same direction as what has been portrayed.

When questions about the effects of viewing television content are simple, they are answered simply. Are there any effects of viewing television content? Yes, on the average, children's information, attitudes, and behaviors are influenced by what they see on television. Ordinarily the influence is in the same direction as that suggested by the television content; occasionally it is in the exact opposite direction. Are the effects of viewing television content any different than the effects of other framed or live experiences with the same content? No, on the average, television's effects are not different from those of other experiences with similar content.

ILLUSTRATIVE RESEARCH ON CONTENT EFFECTS

As it turns out, the research that provides answers for our two simple questions also stimulates debate and suggests that more complex questions and answers may be needed. A detailed review of just a few illustrative studies of television content effects will show how these apparently contradictory consequences of research can all occur at once. The body of work on the effects of exposure to televised aggression is excellent for this purpose, because it is large, varied, and interesting. Examples of every conceivable issue, design, method, and outcome can be found here, and they are no different in character than those found in research on the effects of every other type of content.

Experimental Studies of Behavioral Effects

The granddaddy studies of televised aggression were conducted by the psychologist Albert Bandura and his students beginning in the early 1960s (Bandura, Ross, & Ross, 1961, 1963a, 1963b). These experiments were among the first modern research to demonstrate that children's behavior could be influenced simply by observing others' behavior. Bandura and others were quick to extend the finding to television viewing at home, but his methods were low in ecological validity as the following prototypical example shows:

(1) A preschool child is taken individually from the nursery school classroom by a graduate student researcher.
(2) The child is asked to wait a minute while the researcher finishes up some work.
(3) During the wait the child views a short film containing aggressive actions.
(4) The stimulus is a Super-8 film projected onto the back of a television screen with the sound coming from a tape recorder.

(5) The film shows graduate students playing aggressively and unusually with toys, including climbing atop a large inflated plastic clown doll, punching its nose, and yelling "socko!"
(6) The child is then taken to a small room and invited to play with highly attractive toys.
(7) When the child is fully engaged, she or he is told the toys are too special to play with.
(8) The child is then taken to a playroom that includes the clown doll, guns, bells, other aggressive toys, and nonaggressive toys.
(9) The child is left alone to play for 10 minutes.
(10) The child's actions and vocalizations are recorded by observers hidden behind a one-way window.

The description makes it clear that the experiences provided in Bandura's experiments were not very much like those of everyday life. The "television" viewed bears only a slight resemblance to what children normally watch at home or elsewhere. The viewing situation itself is abnormal. The children's aggressive behaviors are quite natural, but they occur in a rather unusual setting and involve children alone aggressing in play against objects, not people. The opportunity to aggress occurs very soon after viewing someone else with exactly the same toys and right after being frustrated in play with other toys. Since this early work, most research has used more realistic television content, usually all or parts of actual television programs. The outcomes measured, when measurement occurs, and the settings for viewing and behaving vary in naturalness, but many are certainly like everyday life.

The special strength of Bandura's work was that it unambiguously demonstrated that, with the methods used, children's aggressive behavior was influenced by viewing "television" programs in which aggressive behavior was featured. The research designs were always experiments with children randomly assigned to one of three or more groups: children who viewed the film just described, children who viewed a contrasting film or saw live actors, and children who went straight from the nursery school classroom to the special toy playroom. When children's behaviors in the playroom were compared, children who had watched an aggressive film behaved more aggressively than did children who had not watched an aggressive film. They displayed many more aggressive actions and utterances copied from the film and more nonfilm aggressive actions and utterances. The experimental design made the cause of these differences clear.

In a later experiment, 10 preschoolers were matched for home television viewing patterns and then one of each pair was randomly assigned to view regular Saturday morning aggressive cartoons and the other, similar nonaggressive cartoons (Steuer, Applefield, & Smith, 1971). For 10 days before the experimental treatments began, each group spent 10 minutes in a special nursery school playroom equipped with aggressive and nonaggressive toys. Records were kept of their physical interpersonal aggression (hitting, pushing, kicking, squeezing, choking, holding down, and throwing objects at another child). For the next 11 days children viewed the cartoons in their own group and then, again in their own group, played in the special playroom and were observed. Children who watched regular Saturday morning cartoons containing aggressive behavior became more aggressive to their playmates, while children who watched the other cartoons did not change their levels of aggression.

Still later experiments illustrate research with adolescents right where they live (Parke, Berkowitz, Leyens, West, & Sebastian, 1977). Working with delinquent adolescent boys living in special schools, the researchers randomly assigned some living units to an aggressive commercial film group and others to a neutral commercial film group. Boys in each group watched five films on five successive days during which no television viewing was permitted. Their verbal and physical aggression during *everyday* activities was recorded several times a week the three weeks before and the one week of the special films. During the viewing week boys watching aggressive films usually became more aggressive. What happened the next three weeks when normal television viewing resumed and no films were shown differed in the two studies in which it was measured. In one, only the more aggressive boys who watched aggressive films continued to be more aggressive, while in the other only the less aggressive boys who watched aggressive films continued to be more aggressive.

Like Bandura's work, the Parke et al. and Steuer et al. studies used methods that lack some ecological validity. The Steuer et al. study can be faulted because most preschoolers do not have adults taking them out of their regular classrooms, showing them cartoons, and leaving them in a special playroom immediately afterward, nor is the adult in a playroom usually so uninvolved in what the children do there, nor do children usually watch cartoons from which aggression has been edited. The Parke et al. study can be faulted because most adolescents are not delinquent males living in reformatories, nor do teenagers see feature films five days in a row with no opportunity to watch television, nor are feature films the same as television programs.

Despite these shortcomings, most social scientists believe that experimental studies like those just described go a long way toward unambiguously demonstrating that viewing televised aggression can increase subsequent aggressive behavior. Experimental studies that have greater ecological validity, such as those by Parke et al. and Steuer et al., suggest that this phenomenon could occur in everyday life. Further evidence on this point can be obtained from research using nonexperimental designs.

Nonexperimental Studies of Behavioral Effects

Among the many nonexperimental studies of television effects on aggressive behavior, two panel studies stand out (Lefkowitz, Eron, Walder, & Huesmann, 1972; Milavsky, Kessler, Stipp, & Rubens, 1982). In panel studies the television viewing patterns and aggressive behavior of the same group of children (a panel) are measured at two or more points in time. The question, then, is whether variations in children's aggressive behaviors are related to variations in their viewing of aggressive programs. The answer comes from two types of analyses. In one, the relationship between viewing and behavior data from the same point in time is examined to determine if children who watch more aggressive television are also more aggressive. These are termed "concurrent effects." In the other type of analysis, behavior at one point in time is related to viewing at another earlier point in time to determine if children who watch more aggressive television then become more aggressive. These are termed "lagged effects."

The Lefkowitz et al. panel study began with a sample of 875 third-grade boys and girls. Ten years later 427 were recontacted. As a measure of exposure to television violence, participants' three or four favorite television programs were scored for amount of aggression. As a measure of aggressive behavior in school, participants completed a peer nomination measure. For questions such as "Who is always getting into trouble?" and "Who says mean things?" they named as many classmates as they thought appropriate.

Correlations among these four measures (viewing and aggression at third grade and age 19) were then calculated. Four of the six are of interest in a cross-lagged panel correlational analysis strategy like that Lefkowitz et al. used. If the two correlations for viewing and behavior at the same point in time (concurrent effects) are positive and statistically significant, it suggests that viewing and behavior influence each other. A comparison of the lagged correlations is then especially informative. If the correlation between viewing in third grade and aggression at age 19 (lagged effect) is positive and statistically significant, it suggests that viewing television aggression increases aggressive behavior. The alternative, that more aggressive children choose to view more aggressive programs, can be ruled out if the correlation for aggression in third grade and viewing at age 19 (lagged effect) is near zero and significantly different from the other lagged correlation.

The results in the Lefkowitz et al. study are mixed. For girls, there were no relationships between exposure to television violence and aggressive behavior either at the same point in time or from third grade to age 19. There were some relationships for boys. For concurrent effects, television viewing and aggressive behavior were related at third grade but not at age 19. For lagged effects, viewing at third grade and aggressive behavior at age 19 were related and, most importantly, aggressive behavior at third grade and viewing at age 19 were not related. For those wanting to make the case that viewing aggressive television content affects aggressive behavior (and not vice versa) three findings for boys are supportive; all findings for girls and the finding that boys' viewing and behavior at age 19 are not related are not supportive.

The Milavsky et al. study also used a panel design. Instead of cross-lagged panel correlational analyses, they used multiple linear regression analyses of the following basic form: Aggressive behavior at Time T + i is predicted by aggressive behavior at Time T plus exposure to aggressive television at Time T plus some constant. This means that to explain aggressive behavior at one point in time we ask, first, how much that aggression is predicted by aggression at one earlier point in time and, second, how much of the remaining unexplained aggression is predicted by viewing televised aggression at one earlier point in time.

Milavsky et al. studied second through sixth grade boys and girls in two different cities at six different times spaced at increasingly longer intervals over a period of three years. Each time children completed a peer nomination measure of aggressive behavior and a questionnaire indicating how much they had viewed 45 regularly scheduled programs in the past month. The shows were rated for violence, and the exposure measure was calculated taking account of viewing frequency, program length, and violence of content. At each testing, only those grades (up to grade six) with children who had been tested before were included, but all children in the grade were tested whether or not they had participated before. These procedures yielded anywhere from about 175 to about 800 boys (or girls) for each regression analysis. Milavsky et al. also studied a separate sample of adolescent boys, but this work will not be described.

For both boys and girls, the six concurrent correlations between viewing and behavior are all low, positive, and significant whether they are calculated for all boys, for all girls, for those boys or girls whose data were valid by several tests of internal consistency, and for measures corrected for unreliability or not. The highest correlations for boys were obtained with valid reporters whose measures were corrected for unreliability (range of correlations was .104 to .227). The correlations for girls were similar but a little higher. The size of the correlations decreased and some of them became nonsignificant when they were calculated using all children but controlling for race, social class, and quality of reporting by participants.

In the regression analyses for lagged effects, there was little indication that exposure to television violence at Time T predicted much about aggressive behavior at Time T + i when the contribution of aggressive behavior at Time T was first taken into account. Of the 15 regression coefficients for boys for the contribution of viewing television violence to aggressive behavior, 11 are low and positive and three of these are significant. The findings for girls are quite similar.

The Lefkowitz et al. and the Milavsky et al. studies raise considerably more questions than did the experimental studies about the extent to which viewing televised aggression increases subsequent aggressive behavior. In one, there are concurrent and lagged effects for boys but none for girls. In the other, the findings for boys and girls are quite similar, showing some concurrent effects and very few lagged effects. In both, the size of the effects is quite small. In Chapter 5 we will return to some of the questions raised by these findings.

As with the experimental studies, careful researchers recognize limitations to these two nonexperimental studies. The Lefkowitz et al. study can be faulted, because exposure to televised violence was represented simply by violence of favorite programs; because the 19-year-olds were judging peers' aggressive behavior as they remembered it at least a year earlier; because reports by oneself, one's mother, or one's peers may not accurately represent what one actually does; because one can never be absolutely certain that the lost participants (of which there were a large number) and the retained participants are really the same; because the cross-lagged panel correlational analysis technique imposes certain restrictions on the quality of the data and the theoretical model that the Lefkowitz et al. study probably cannot meet; and because the analysis technique itself may be weaker than others that could be used (see Kenny, 1972; Milavsky et al., 1982; and Neale, 1972 for further discussion). The Milavsky et al. study can also be faulted, because it used reports by oneself and one's peers to stand for actual behavior; because of unresolvable concern that lost participants are somehow different from those retained in the sample; because some controls entered in the concurrent correlations may not be appropriate; and because the particular model used for the multiple linear regression analyses represents only one of several ways in which lagged effects could occur (see Comstock, in press; Cook, Kendzierski, & Thomas, 1983; and Kenny, 1984, for further discussion).

Despite these shortcomings, most social scientists believe that nonexperimental studies like those just described provide important evidence about the short-term and long-term relationships between viewing televised violence and behaving aggressively in everyday life. When considered with the findings from experimental research, they suggest that the effects of exposure to television violence are attenuated in everyday life as compared to the laboratory. Long-term effects are particularly weak or even nonexistent.

Studies of Informational and Attitudinal Effects

Like studies of behavioral effects of television content, studies of informational and attitudinal effects also use experimental and nonexperimental designs with varying degrees of ecological validity. Structurally, the research is just the same. The variations in informational and attitudinal measures of effects of exposure are also just as great as those for behavioral measures. A brief review of the kinds of outcomes measured in the area of aggression, in conjunction with knowledge of the research designs and methods already described, should provide a good feel for work on these effects.

Research on television content effects on children's information about aggression has measured such outcomes as knowledge of the verbal and physical aggression performed in the program they saw, ideas about how aggressive taxi drivers are, ideas about the frequency of various crimes in American communities, and ideas about how violent strangers are likely to be. With measures such as these, informational effects are sometimes not found and, where they are found, the "information" children have acquired is sometimes an inaccurate representation of reality. Most often, however, informational effects are found, and they are in the direction of learning whatever accurate or inaccurate information television presents.

Research on effects on attitudes about aggression also includes several different types of outcome measures. For example, studies have assessed children's opinions about the acceptability of aggressive resolutions to interpersonal conflict, attitudes about the use of physical force by law enforcement officers, positive and negative evaluations of characters who vary in how aggressive they are, and acceptance of aggressive behaviors in themselves. Again, it should be emphasized that, with measures such as these, attitudinal effects are sometimes not found and that, when effects are found, they are not always in the direction of encouraging the most socially acceptable attitudes about aggression. Nonetheless, the measures are representative of the kinds of attitudinal effects that have been studied.

Studies Comparing Television to Other Sources

Compared to research investigating whether television content has any effect at all, there is little work investigating whether television's effects are any different than those of other potential sources of influence. Even in the immense literature on television aggression there are few studies comparing television's impact on aggression to the impact of such other experiences with similar aggressive content as listening to the radio, reading books, watching a movie, watching peers, interacting with siblings, or watching parents. From the small number available, the illustration we will choose comes, once again, from the body of research conducted by Bandura and his students.

In an early study of the determinants of aggressive behavior, Bandura, Ross, and Ross (1963a) compared the impacts of a live person performing aggressive acts right in the same room, that same live person performing the same acts in a "television" program, and that same person performing the same acts in a "television" program in which the person dressed as a cat and added catlike embellishments to the behaviors. The design was experimental, with preschool children randomly assigned to one of the three experimental conditions or a control condition. The methods were very similar to those described earlier. Results showed that children's total aggressive behaviors were equally affected by the live human, the filmed human, and the filmed cat and were much more frequent than the aggressive behaviors of children in the control condition.

Some nonexperimental studies have compared the effects of television on aggression to the effects of other experiences. The Milavsky et al. (1982) study, for instance, reported concurrent correlations between boys' and girls' aggressive behavior and their viewing television violence, reading violent comic books, seeing violent movies, having aggressive friends, being students in aggressive classrooms, and at least 20 other such experiences. The largest correlations were with children's friends and classmates, next their parents, next television, and last other media.

The meaning of differences in these correlations is problematic. One can say they demonstrate that in everyday life televised aggression is not very influential compared to peers and parents. Alternatively, one can say that the differences are uninterpretable because each experience was measured on a different metric and involved different aggressive content. The television violence exposure measure represented hours of viewing weighted by violence of content viewed for four weeks. The movie violence exposure measure was simply how many of four violent movies then in local theaters students said they had seen. The mother's use of physical punishment measure was the sum of her responses to five questions about the likelihood of hitting, slapping, or spanking her child for different infractions and one question about the total number of times she used physical punishment in the last year. It is clear from just these three measures that different types and amounts of experiences are being compared here. Some would say this provides no basis for deciding whether television has the same impact as other experiences with similar content for the same amount of time. Where, however, in everyday life would one ever find children who clearly obtained from some experience other than television viewing the same amount of experience with aggression like that presented on television? And, if these children were found, how likely is it that they would not also watch aggression on television? Experimental designs are necessary here.

Summary

The illustrative studies in this section serve as prototypical examples of all research on the effects of television content on children. They clarify what experimental and nonexperimental designs and more and less ecologically valid methods look like;

what kinds of informational, attitudinal, and behavioral effects are explored; and how researchers investigate the two questions of whether there are any television effects at all and whether television effects differ from those of other experiences with aggression. The body of research on television and aggression is so large that it has at least one example of virtually every type of television content effects research ever done. The body of work for all other content areas is much smaller. Whatever content area one turns to, however, will only contain research like that described here for aggression.

TELEVISION AND CHILDREN'S WELL-BEING

What then can we say in response to parents' and social commentators' concerns about the television content children can view? Is television today the powerful framed experience excoriated by Hayakawa and so worthy of the social control Plato advocated? Should parents decide what their children watch on television, encouraging children to watch certain programs and forbidding them to watch others? Should schools invest in television and produce programs to instruct students in reading, writing, and arithmetic?

The process of formulating answers to these questions must begin with evidence about the effects of television content on children. Research shows that television content *can* affect children's information, attitudes, and behaviors. The effect is not really limited to particular types of content: Positive and negative content is effective; content intended primarily to inform, instruct, persuade, or entertain is effective; live action, animated, allegorical, and literal content is effective; and content aimed at instilling, enhancing, or changing information, beliefs, skills, feelings, attitudes, and behaviors is all effective. The effect is not really limited to particular viewing situations: Viewing at home alone, at home with others, in school, at a friend's house, or in a research laboratory is effective. The effect is not even limited to particular children: Effects have been demonstrated for children of both sexes, many racial and ethnic groups, different social classes, many religions, different geographical regions, all levels of intelligence, and many social and psychological adjustment levels. There is little doubt that all those who praise or criticize television content are right in their belief that television can present content that makes a desirable or undesirable contribution to children's well-being.

Unfortunately, there is also little doubt, given what most children watch on television, that the critics are right to be concerned about television content (see Singer & Singer, 1983, for recent statement). This is not to say that television content per se is bad for children or that television only broadcasts content that is bad for children. Rather it is to say that of the 25 to 35 hours of television American children watch each week most was not designed with children's welfare in mind, and some of it is decidedly aggressive, sexist, ageist, racist, consumption oriented, sexy, inane, or moronic. Little of what children watch is truly uplifting, visionary, educational, or informative. Parents and critics have reason to be concerned about television's role in children's lives and to think about controlling what is broadcast and/or what is watched. At the very least, they can lament all the good opportunities television wastes and guide children's viewing toward what is good and away from what is bad.

Having decided that there is some empirical basis for suggesting that social controls should be placed on what is broadcast into the home, that parents should guide children's viewing, and that schools should use television for instruction, the question arises as to the strength of the evidence. The research examples in this chapter show that the evidentiary base has some cracks in it. Weaker effects are obtained when more ecologically valid methods are employed and when long-term or more generalized effects are sought. In any given study, only some children are affected by television content. These cracks in our empirical evidence about the effects of television content on children have led to significant debate among researchers, social commentators, parents, broadcasters, and policy makers about how important a force television content really is in the everyday lives of children.

5

REFINING THE VIEW OF TELEVISION CONTENT EFFECTS

Arguments abound about the size of any television content effects in everyday life, the generality of these effects, and the characteristics of the affected children, but the debates can be reduced with more precise, complex theoretical models of the effects process.

A few simple facts have led to much debate about the real significance of television content in children's everyday lives and to progressively more elaborated theories to explain how and when television content effects occur. Television content can affect children. Television content effects are not found in every study. Where found, effects never apply to every child participating in the study. And where found, effects are rarely of enormous size or generality. These facts form the background from which arise the important issues of the day, the major debates in the field.

DEBATES ABOUT EFFECTS OF TELEVISION CONTENT

There are three areas of significant debate about the effects of television content on children: the size of the effects, the specificity of the effects, and the characteristics of the affected population. The position one takes in each debate is dependent not only on the available evidence but also on one's model of how television functions in children's lives, and it has important implications for one's stance toward formal and informal regulation of television content. A review of the debates will show how each side uses existing data, illustrate the limits of our knowledge about the effects of television content on children, demonstrate how theory and policy are intertwined in the debates, and indicate fruitful avenues for future research (see Comstock, 1983, in press, for other reviews).

Effect Size

We said that some researchers argue that television content has no effects on children but that most researchers believe there are some effects. Many of those who claim that exposure to television content has no effects on children are really saying that the size, consistency, generality, and/or ecological validity of the effects are sufficiently small that effects are functionally nonexistent in children's everyday lives. They do not usually question the validity of those studies that show some effect of exposure to television content; rather, they question whether any appreciable effect occurs in the real world in which children ordinarily watch television and behave.

When a researcher claims that exposure to television content has an effect on children's information, attitudes, or behaviors, he or she is saying either that there is a statistically significant difference between groups in an experimental design or that there is a statistically significant association between amount of exposure and amount of outcome in a nonexperimental design. This is a statistical claim that says that the group differences or associations are highly unlikely to have occurred by chance. In order to make this type of claim it turns out that group differences or associations do not necessarily have to be very large.

This becomes apparent if we look closely at some effects in the illustrative studies described in Chapter 4. In the Lefkowitz et al. (1972) work, the statistically significant associations between preferences for violent television programs in the third grade and aggressive behavior either in the third grade or at age 19 account for 4% to 10% of all variability in aggressive behavior at either time. That leaves about 90% of all aggressive behavior arising from causes other than exposure to television violence. In the Milavsky et al. (1982) work, the few significant concurrent correlations between television viewing and aggressive behavior account for 2% to 10% of the variability in aggressive behavior, with most of them accounting for only 2% to 5% of the variability.

Experimental studies are not usually analyzed so that one can talk about the amount of variability accounted for by exposure to particular television content; however, a review of the size of group differences is instructive. In the Steuer et al. (1971) study, during each 10-minute play session the experimental and control pairs differed by as few as none and as many as 30 aggressive behaviors. In Study 1 of the Parke et al. (1977) series, the largest experimental versus control group difference was about 0.1 more aggressive acts per 30-second interval.

Effect sizes such as these are fairly representative of those found in other research on television content effects. Experimental designs in which statistically significant group differences are found usually show actual group differences that range from the socially trivial to the somewhat important but not earth shaking. Non-experimental designs usually produce associations between exposure to television content and the outcome of interest that account for no more than about 10% of the variability in the outcome measure, leaving at least 90% of the variability in that measure attributable to other influences.

Most people agree these findings indicate that television content can sometimes appreciably affect children under carefully controlled experimental conditions, but they disagree about their implications for television content effects in children's everyday lives. Some argue that exposure to television content accounts for a socially insignificant, even meaningless amount (from 0% to 5%!) of children's information, attitudes, and behaviors in their everyday lives and that the absolute differences in knowledge, attitudes, or behaviors between those who watch a lot and a little of any content are either nonexistent or so small as to be socially irrelevant. Others argue that the amount of variability in an outcome measure that can be attributed to television content is about the same size as the amount attributable to schools or parents and that identifying the cause of even 5% of the variability is important. Moreover, they believe that correct theory recognizes that any single socialization agent (e.g., television or schools or parents) should not ordinarily be a preeminent or sole determinant of children's information, attitudes, or behaviors. Finally, they point to the more ecologically valid field experiments (e.g., Friedrich & Stein, 1973; Parke et al., 1977) as providing strong empirical support for the assertion that exposure to everyday television content in everyday circumstances can produce measurable, and therefore important, differences in children's everyday behaviors in everyday settings.

Effect Specificity

This debate centers on the extent to which television content effects are limited to a few very specific circumstances. It usually focuses on the extent to which the measured outcome is a copy of what was presented on television or a generalization of it, the extent to which the measurement situation is a copy of what was presented on television or a generalization of it, and the extent to which measured effects occur immediately after viewing or sometime later. The debate is about the circumstances under which effects of any size are likely to be found and the social significance of these circumstances; it is not a debate about the size of the effects.

On one side of the debate are those claiming that television content effects appear only when the measured outcomes and the measurement setting are very similar to those presented in the television content and measurement occurs virtually immediately after viewing (see Freedman, 1984, for recent statement). The strongest and most consistent evidence for television content effects comes, they claim, from modeling studies such as Bandura's in which imitation is assessed soon after viewing in circumstances very like those presented in the television content. They do not usually assert that these very specific effects are also ecologically invalid. They recognize that everyday television presents specific acts that can influence viewers in their everyday lives; for instance, a runaway teenager calling home after seeing such an event in a made-for-television movie or a child indiscriminately stuffing food in her mouth like Cookie Monster. They view specific effects with alarm or delight, depending on the effect, but they do not therefore conclude that the effects of television content are socially significant. They argue instead that because television content effects are highly specific, they are very infrequent and limited to a very few, probably unusual, viewers.

On the other side of the debate are those claiming either that measured effects have been obtained under less severely limited conditions or that even these limited effects are socially significant. They point to studies such as those by Steuer et al. (1971), Parke et al. (1977), and Lefkowitz et al. (1972) as indicating that everyday television content can affect children in their everyday lives. They are apt to agree that the strongest television content effects are found under the most specific conditions, but they argue that there is ample evidence for more generalized effects. They also consider specific effects in everyday life—the runaway calling home and the food being strewn on the floor—to be socially significant even if limited to a few children.

Affected Population's Characteristics

This third debate centers on the extent to which television content effects occur for all children or only a selected group. It is a debate about whether television has effects only for those children who are emotionally deprived, socially maladjusted, highly aggressive, or otherwise unusual in their characteristics, or small in number. It is not a debate about whether any one piece of content, type of content, or viewing pattern will produce effects in *all* children.

Statistically significant research results do not apply consistently to each and every child who participates in the research, nor do they apply to each and every child for whom one would like to predict outcomes. The Steuer et al. (1971) study described in Chapter 4 clearly illustrates the common finding that, even when there are statistically significant differences between experimental groups, these differences do not apply to every individual participant. For example, for Pair 5 the experimental and control group children were equally aggressive. Moreover, the Pair 2 experimental child probably did not differ in aggressive behavior from the Pair 3 control child and maybe even from the Pair 4 control child. Thus, a general finding that exposure to aggressive Saturday morning cartoons increases interpersonal aggression during play does not also mean that every child who views aggressive Saturday morning cartoons will become more aggressive than any child who does not watch such cartoons. Similarly, for nonexperimental research, the finding of a statistically significant association between exposure and outcome does not mean that the relationship holds for every child.

Having accepted as incontrovertible the fact that no television content affects all children, the question arises as to which children are affected by television content. Are some children more swayed by television than others? Are some children always ready to adopt ideas in certain content areas, such as aggression or computer programming? If there are certain children who are always vulnerable to television content effects or to content effects in certain areas and other children who are never influenced by television, then one might say that certain children use television and that television never uses children. There would then be no television content effects created solely by television; there would only be television content effects created by certain children using what television provided. To support this position one needs to show that content effects are consistently limited to certain children.

To date, no one has successfully isolated personal characteristics, proclivities, or circumstances that invariably identify in advance (or separate after the fact) those children who will be (or have been) influenced by television content from those who will not be (or have not been) influenced. A recent review of the voluminous research literature on televised aggression found little evidence that *only* certain types of children were influenced (Dorr & Kovaric, 1980). There was a suggestion that more aggressive boys and girls are more likely to be influenced by aggressive television content, as illustrated in some of the Parke et al. (1977) studies, and perhaps that children between the ages of 8 and 12 are more likely than younger or older children to be influenced. In general, however, there are no strong empirical grounds for claiming that only children with certain characteristics are influenced by aggressive television content. The same conclusions can be drawn for all other content areas in which there is enough research to test the proposition that only certain types of children are ever affected by television or by particular television content.

Resolving the Debates

All three debates about the effects of television content on children involve elements of theory, evidence, and values. The debates can be reduced in scope by relying on evidence from well-chosen and methodologically correct research. We may one day understand how much any single socialization agent influences children's information, attitudes, and behaviors and thus be able to use that as a standard against which to measure the significance of television content as a socialization agent. We may also someday decide how large a change in information, attitudes, or behaviors must be to be socially important and thus be able to evaluate the impact that television has on what children know, believe, and do. Similarly, we can develop a body of research that will allow us to estimate better the extent to which content effects only occur soon after viewing and are limited to outcomes and circumstances that are quite similar to those televised. And we can more fully test the proposition that only certain types of children are ever influenced by television content or by television content dealing only with certain topics. Finally, we may one day understand how less ecologically valid methods relate to phenomena in everyday life and thus be able to judge the significance of a sizable portion of our present research accordingly.

Ultimately, however, there will be a residue of debate that hinges on values that are not subject to empirical evidence, values that at present figure strongly in the debates. Television will never be found to be all-powerful. We will each have to decide how much effect of what kind for whom is important. Values will surely influence the decisions at which we arrive, but an abundance of high quality empirical evidence and valid theory will reduce the scope of our future debates.

In the meantime we can turn to an analysis of what is now known about the processes by which television content affects children and the several factors that influence whether or not television content effects occur. These involve a confluence of factors emanating from the characteristics of the television content, the characteristics of the viewers, the characteristics of the setting, and the interplays among them. Taken together, they help account for the limitations we have seen in the size and generality of television content effects and in the number and type of viewers affected, and they provide a basis for some rough predictions about what content will affect which viewers in which circumstances.

MODELS AND VARIABLES FOR THE EFFECTS PROCESS

It may seem unusual to the experienced reader of social science literature to discuss theoretical models and variables after discussing content effects research that presumably embodies such theory. But much research about television content effects on children is motivated more by an interest in social phenomena, child welfare, and/or social policy than by an interest in developing and testing theory. It emphasizes unambiguous causal inference and ecological validity over theory. To be sure, theoretical models and variables are always borrowed as convenient or necessary, and some researchers clearly begin with a strong theoretical base, but theory building is probably not the primary motivation for the majority of television content effects studies. Nonetheless, good theory could contribute much to our understanding of such effects in everyday life.

Theoretical explanations for the transaction between television content and children range along a continuum that at one end places primary power in the television content and at the other end places it in the child. The first studies of television content effects, those of the psychologist Albert Bandura and his colleagues in the 1960s, took the former approach. Since then, Bandura has moved a long way toward the other end, where other theoreticians have begun. Each theoretical perspective has led researchers to investigate a certain set of variables more than others. We will turn to the important television, child, and setting variables each has identified after a brief review of the major theoretical models proposed to account for the transactions between television content and children.

Theoretical Models

Effects models that place primary emphasis on television go by names such as *catharsis theory, cultivation theory,* and *social learning theory.* None was developed solely to explain how television content comes to affect children, but we will limit the description of each theory to this particular situation. All three theories begin with television content as the stimulus to which children are exposed. Children look and listen to what television presents and are affected by whatever is most clearly and cogently presented. According to catharsis theory, viewing of content that addresses primary psychological drives (such as aggression or sex) allows children then and there to discharge the energy associated with these drives and thereby have less of this energy to discharge in subsequent interactions with other people. According to cultivation theory, frequent viewing of content that inevitably reflects a certain world view cultivates such a world view in children who watch television. According to social learning theory, also sometimes known as *observational learning theory* and *modeling theory,* viewing any content leads children to reproduce this content when there is good reason to reproduce it in their environment. The reproductions may be exact copies (sitting on the bobo doll and punching its nose), reasonable facsimiles (slapping the bobo doll's nose without sitting on it), or broad generalizations (pushing a friend who tries to take a toy).

Catharsis theory was described in Chapter 4. To review briefly, the theory proposes that viewing a drama in which powerful human emotions are represented and acted upon serves to decrease the reservoir of such emotions in the viewer (Feshbach, 1955, 1961; Feshbach & Singer, 1971). The focus is on those emotions that are powerful motivators of behavior but whose behavioral expression needs to be closely controlled in interpersonal interactions. While anger and its expression in aggressive behavior are probably the most frequently studied, other possibilities include sexuality, hedonism, avarice, and the like. According to the theory, a child who watches television programs in which interpersonal aggression is featured will subsequently be less aggressive in everyday life than he or she would otherwise be. Catharsis is a theory for which there is very little research support in the social science literature.

Cultivation theory seeks to explain how television content influences children's mental images of the world in which they live. Its major proponent has been the communications theorist George Gerbner, with assistance from his colleagues and students (Gerbner & Gross, 1980; Gerbner, Gross, Morgan, & Signorielli, 1980). The theory focuses on television content conveying ideas about social behavior, social norms, and social structure and on the effects of such content on children's beliefs about their society. It asserts that most of children's television viewing presents them with a consistent view of society in programs that influence in a process similar to erosion or cultivation. Television, for example, regularly shows women whose only occupation is wife and mother, who have no obvious occupation, or who have an occupation outside the home but rarely seem to work at it. The effects process for this content begins with a single viewing, but the effects occur only a bit at a time. Each viewing adds a little more effect, but no single viewing produces an easily measured effect. Rather, much like erosion or cultivation, effects can only be seen when the process has had a considerable opportunity to operate, and variations in effects can only be seen in comparisons of children with sizable differences in their viewing habits. Eventually, children who view a lot will have more traditional images of women as homemakers, to carry the example through, than will children who view a little.

Social learning has been most interested in developing a model of the process by which television influences children's behavior (Bandura, 1973, 1977, 1978). In the heyday of behaviorism, social learning theorists began by demonstrating that children could be influenced vicariously, that direct instruction, experience, and reinforcement were not necessary for children to acquire information about behavior or for them to enhance or change their own behaviors. In contrast to catharsis theory, in social learning theory exposure to particular content is supposed to lead to more such content in the child's information, attitudes, or behaviors. In contrast to cultivation theory, the effect can occur after only one viewing. The effect may be a direct copy or imitation of what was presented on television or it may be different but in the same class or category.

Once social learning theorists had convincingly shown that behavioral effects could occur simply because a child once viewed a televised action he or she could understand and perform in his or her environment, their attention turned to delineating the characteristics of television content and environments for which such vicarious effects were more and less likely. Step by step since it was first formulated in the early 1960s, social learning theory has been elaborated and enlarged. The first efforts emphasized the contributions of specific characteristics of the television content (e.g., how much aggression is rewarded) and of the setting for measuring outcomes (e.g., how similar it is to the television setting) to determining the effects of television content on children. Later refinements emphasized the role of viewers' needs, interests, abilities, motivations, and self concepts in the process model. Bandura, in fact, now calls his much-revised theory *social cognitive theory.*

Another psychologist, Leonard Berkowitz (1962, 1973), has proposed an effects model that also focuses on behavioral outcomes and now involves many cognitive elements as well. It is most applicable to older adolescents and adults, who think well and already know a lot about their world. The theory has been developed especially to deal with effects on socially sanctioned behaviors such as aggression. *Cognitive neo-associationism,* as it is called, proposes that seeing aggression on television loosens controls a viewer holds on his or her aggression. In technical terms, it disinhibits aggression. Disinhibition is greater if the televised aggression is shown as justified or acceptable to others. Once disinhibited, aggressive acts are more likely to be performed in everyday life, but there is no expectation these acts will be exact imitations of the acts seen on television. They will just be the same type or class of behavior. The likelihood of some aggressive act also increases as the cues in everyday life become more similar to those on television. If the television victim of aggression had the same name as the person insulting you in real life, according to the theory you will be more likely to aggress than if the victim had a different name.

A very different type of model postulates that television content has the effects it does because of its energizing and de-energizing effects. The two major proponents of this view have been the communications scholars Percy Tannenbaum and Dolf Zillmann (Tannenbaum & Zillmann, 1975). According to the model, aggressive content, for instance, arouses viewers, increasing their store of energy or excitation. After viewing, this energy will be fed into whatever activity they first have the opportunity to perform. If it is an instigation to aggress, viewers will be more aggressive than those who have not just seen arousing television content.

Process models that begin by focusing on the child go by such names as *constructivism* or *phenomenology* and *uses and gratifications.* Neither approach was developed solely to explain children's transactions with television content, but our descriptions of each theory will be limited to this special case. Both theories begin with the child actively engaged in making sense of and in operating in his or her world. As a part of that world, television offers the child information, entertainment, persuasion, relaxation, and escape depending on how the child chooses to interpret and relate to television content. In the constructivist model, one can only understand what a child will do with television if one knows how that particular child made sense of the television content and probably knows as well the child's personality and living circumstances. In the uses and gratifications approach, one can understand what a child will do with television if one knows what motivated the child to view television.

The constructivist model (or phenomenology) was described in Chapter 2 (J. Anderson, 1981, 1983). It is an approach to understanding human behavior that emphasizes children's active determination of their experiences and that recognizes and relishes individuality and diversity. It assumes that children strive to make sense of their world and to operate successfully in it. It also assumes that children are sensitive and receptive to information that helps them develop useful, productive understandings of their world. This suggests that television content could affect children because they would choose to treat it as meaningful and useful information. But it does not lead one to study television content effects per se. There are no such effects, except as children determine them. Phenomenology by itself provides no basis for studying television content effects in any of the ways that were described in Chapter 4, even if it is a model adopted by some in an effort to understand children's interactions with television content.

The uses and gratifications approach, on the other hand, offers a basis for specifying which children will be affected when by which content (Blumler & Katz, 1974). It emphasizes that children actively choose the experiences in which they will engage. These choices are governed by the gratifications children anticipate receiving from experiences. Any particular television program and television viewing per se can offer more than one gratification to viewers, or put another way it can serve several functions. For instance, one child may view a situation comedy in order to escape from the rigors of an argumentative household, while another child may watch the same program in order to learn more about how children can express love to their parents, and a third child may watch in order to be amused.

According to the model, children are not limited to experiencing one and only one gratification from a particular television viewing experience nor are they limited to always using television for the same set of gratifications. Moreover, gratifications obtained from television viewing may also be obtained from other activities. Emphasis is on the reasons why children choose to view television rather than do something else and, having chosen to view, why they choose one program over others. Children's motivations for choosing are expected to relate to the television content effects that occur. For example, children who watch a family situation comedy to get ideas about how other families handle disagreements are more likely to learn such techniques than are children who watch the same comedy to avoid doing homework.

There is now enough research about the effects of television content on children to know that no theoretical explanation will be adequate if it focuses solely on television content or solely on the child viewer. As a research strategy, a singular focus can be quite productive, because it can clarify how variations in television content or in children predict variations in outcomes. However, a complete model must include both and must locate them in settings that will themselves influence the interactions of children and television.

We do not yet have a complete model of how the transaction between television content and children occurs. Social learning is the theory most often used in studying television content effects. Over the years the theory has moved from a primary emphasis on television content to a primary emphasis on the child. There is no way now to predict what the most adequate theory of the future will look like exactly. The research we have now suggests that it will have to include several television content, child viewer, and setting variables singly and in integrated interaction with each other.

Television Content Variables

There are several television content variables that influence children. Many have been identified by those interested in designing effective instructional programs, while others have been identified by those interested in commercial and public television's effects on children's social attitudes and behaviors. Those studying instructional programs could usually use stimuli very much like everyday school television. The others have often used specially constructed, not terribly realistic materials, both because it is prohibitively expensive to create research materials that are as well done as everyday television programs and because everyday television programs rarely manipulate the variables of interest to these researchers.

Together, these two types of studies, using different kinds of television material, suggest numerous variables that predict how much influence content will have on children (for earlier summaries see Leifer, 1976, and Schramm, 1972). These variables are most easily presented in a list with a short explanation for each item:

(1) *Repetition.* Content that is repeated more often within the same program, across a set of programs, or in repeated viewing of one program is more likely to have an effect.

(2) *Clarity.* Ideas that are clearly presented in logical order without extraneous material, interruptions, or conflicting ideas are more likely to have an effect.

(3) *Encodability.* Content that is presented with a visual and verbal style that is easily understood and easily translated into words for storage in memory is more likely to have an effect.
(4) *Familiarity.* Content that contains more elements already familiar to children is more likely to have an effect.
(5) *Participation.* Content that leads viewers to participate actively in rehearsing it during viewing is more likely to have an effect.
(6) *Reinforcement.* Content for which some positive reinforcement occurs in the program when the content is presented is more likely to have an effect.
(7) *Status.* Content that is associated with higher status, more socially valued protagonists, situations, or outcomes is more likely to have an effect.
(8) *Identification.* Content that permits children to identify with principal characters because they are similar to the children or embody characteristics to which children aspire is more likely to have an effect.
(9) *Variation.* Content that is presented in several different guises, with different protagonists, and in different situations is more likely to have an effect.
(10) *Realism.* Content that is presented as real or realistic is more likely to have an effect.
(11) *Arousal.* Content that is presented in a program context that provokes moderate arousal in viewers is more likely to have an effect.

Two implications can be drawn from this list. The first, and most important, is that content is a crucial element in the model of the transactions between television and children. The research from which the list of variables was constructed clearly shows that variations in television content by themselves affect children's information, attitudes, or behaviors after viewing. Thus, television content uses children. The second implication is that television content effects will vary as the content itself varies on these variables. Here, then, is a means to begin to specify when television content effects should be larger and when smaller and when they should be more general and when more specific. With these variables we have a leg up on resolving the debates about the size and specificity of television content effects.

Child Viewer Variables

Many of the 11 television content variables only become influential when a child viewer makes them operative. For instance, scripted reinforcement to a child actor who looks both ways before crossing the street can only operate as vicarious reinforcement when the child viewer understands that the actor looked both ways before crossing the street, that the actor's friend's subsequent actions were positive, and that the friend's positive actions were elicited by the actor looking both ways before crossing the street. As explained in Chapters 2 and 3, children construct meaning for the television content others produce and broadcast. Producers can fashion content so as to increase or decrease the likelihood of children constructing particular meanings for it, but child viewers cast the deciding ballots about what any content means and thereby influence the kinds of effects content can have on them.

Children also influence television content effects according to their interests and needs in the content area. As described in the section "Affected Population's Characteristics," there is some evidence, particularly in the areas of aggression and social attitudes, that those children who demonstrate more of the expected outcome prior to viewing are more influenced by the content. Presumably this is because they are more interested in such content, pay more attention to it when it is broadcast, and take its messages more seriously. Indeed, as suggested in Chapter 3, there have been several demonstrations that those children who are more interested in a topic prior to exposure usually learn more from a television program about it. More generally, it can be said that children's reasons for watching television programs partially predict the effects of the programs on them.

Another child viewer variable, one introduced in Chapters 2 and 3 and one to which we will return in Chapter 7, is how knowledgeable children are about the television medium. Those who understand more about how and why the content they are watching was produced and broadcast are more likely to moderate its effects based on their assessments of how much the content is biased, factual, persuasive, informative, realistic, fantastic, constructed, or live. When children understand, for example, that an advertisement is produced to present a product in its very best light and to persuade viewers to want it, they are somewhat less likely to be persuaded by the commercial. When children believe that a campus riot story is factual, they are somewhat more likely to increase their own aggressiveness after viewing.

Foremost among the child viewer variables from a developmentalist's perspective is age. Age, however, is nothing more than a rather gross indicator of different viewers' information-processing, interpretive and evaluative abilities, knowledge of the social and physical world, needs, interests, abilities to control themselves and manage their activities, and established patterns of thought, feeling, and action. Age-related differences in these areas, some of which were reviewed in Chapter 3, suggest contingent differences in the effects of television content. Because children become better able to understand and remember television content as they mature, they have more opportunity to be affected by it. Because older children know more, have greater self control, and have more established behavioral patterns, they should be less affected and/or more differentially affected. Because children's interests and needs change, the types of program content that are influential should change. These are important predictions that are completely compatible with what is known about children and what influences them.

Few of these notions have been well tested in a single research study involving children of different ages. My former colleague, the communications researcher Donald Roberts, and I once did (Leifer & Roberts, 1972). We showed entertainment programs to kindergartners and third, sixth, ninth, and twelfth graders. The programs varied in the amount of violence and aggression portrayed. Kindergartners' postviewing aggression was somewhat influenced by the amount of aggression in the programs. Third graders' aggression was very much influenced. The amount of influence then gradually decreased for the older students until twelfth graders' aggression was not at all influenced by the programs. For every grade where any effect showed up, the effect was always the same: The more aggression and violence in the program, the more aggressive the students after viewing. How much more aggressive depended on the viewer's age.

One can imagine that the age of maximum influence of television would change when researchers used a completely different type of content, say romantic love or postholocaust society or nursery school life, and when that content was presented in different formats. It is fascinating to speculate how age-related variations in knowledge, ability, inclination, and relevance operate to determine television content effects. More research is needed, however, before the interplay of the complex of age-related factors can be sensibly spelled out.

Finding, as we have, that variations in children are associated with variations in apparent television content effects confirms the need to include the child in any complete model of the transaction between television content and the child. Television may use children, but just as surely children use television. The constructivist perspective described in Chapter 2 has come back, even if only as part of the whole picture. Those embracing constructivist, phenomenological, and uses and gratifications perspectives are right to insist that these perspectives have much to offer to our understanding of the role television content plays in children's lives. The variables described here suggest some of the ways in which these perspectives ought to be represented in a complete model. In addition, they provide a means for beginning to specify which viewers will be affected when, thereby resolving some of the issues raised in the debate about which children are affected by television content.

Setting Variables

The third set of variables operating in the television content effects process has been called, for want of a better term, *setting variables.* Children's life circumstances differ in ways that make some children more likely than others to find television content relevant to their lives and to encounter opportunities or inducements to put television content into use. Setting variables specify what those circumstances are.

As noted in the section "Effect Specificity," there is some evidence that television effects are demonstrated more often in settings that are more similar to those depicted on television and in settings that encourage the same type of information, attitude, or behavior as depicted on television. For example, circumstances that encourage or condone aggressive behavior (e.g., rewarding children for demonstrating aggression they have seen on television or putting children in competition in a room where the adult does not monitor or respond to children's behaviors) are more likely to elicit aggressive behavior than are other settings. Similarly, taking two children to a small room and asking them to draw one picture using one piece of paper and three colored markers is more likely to produce the cooperative behaviors they have seen in a similar television segment than is having them join a group of children playing outdoors. Thus, certain settings can enhance the likelihood that television content effects will be demonstrated by children.

Rather different settings apparently enhance the likelihood that television content will be accepted at all by children, whether or not it is demonstrated. These settings are most different from those in which children carry out their everyday lives. The communications researcher Robert Hornik and his colleagues have articulated this idea especially well (Hornik, Gonzalez, & Gould, 1980). They argue that television content is most likely to be accepted by children when it involves people, actions, places, and times with which children are unfamiliar in their everyday lives, what Hornik et al. call "distant environments." Thus, television would be an especially influential source of images about blacks for those white children who live in highly segregated white settings. It is also most likely to become a source of ideas about foreign countries never visited, schools never attended, and workplaces never entered.

Hornik et al.'s proposition about distant environments is related to the notion advanced in Chapter 4 that it is easier for children to acquire than to enhance or change information, attitudes, or behaviors based on what they see on television. Because children know little or nothing about distant environments, the only effect television content can have is that of acquisition. Since acquisition is the easiest effect to obtain, television content about distant environments should be more readily accepted than content about topics children already know about. Such learning cannot, however, be put into action unless the child enters the distant environment or one similar to it. The findings about how settings affect the likelihood children will accept television content and put it into action in their everyday lives can be helpful in resolving some of the debates about the specificity of television content effects and the characteristics of affected populations.

Summary

Television content, child viewer, and setting variables predict television content effects. This reaffirms the wisdom of choosing a middle ground in a theoretical explanation of the transaction between television content and children. It also suggests a need to reformulate the television content effects questions posed in Chapter 4. "Does television content have an effect?" is too grand a question, even if it is the question everyone first wants to answer. "Does television have the same effect as other means for delivering the same content?" is too simple a question, even if the answer helps decide how to instruct students or where to buy advertising time.

We need to revise our central questions so that they better reflect the complexities of life. The simplest versions of the revised questions would be "Under what circumstances does television content affect which children?" and "Under what circumstances does television affect children differently than other means of delivering the same content?" The material reviewed in this section provides many of the specifications for *what* television content will affect *which* children in *what* settings and *how* these effects will compare to the effects of other means of delivering the same content. We do not yet know enough to understand fully the role of television content in children's lives nor how television compares to other sources of influence, but the processes and variables identified thus far help delineate when television is likely to play any part in any children's lives.

TELEVISION AND CHILDREN'S WELL-BEING REVISITED

What can we say now in response to parents' and social commentators' concerns about the television content children can view? Should we control what television content is broadcast? Should parents control what their children watch? Should schools use television as a means of instruction?

The answers to these questions do not depend entirely on the extent to which children will acquire, enhance, or change their information, attitudes, or behaviors because of what they have watched on television. Deciding to exert social control over framed experiences also involves issues of free speech, free enterprise, and cost. Deciding to control home viewing also involves issues of available alternative activities for children and parental disciplinary stamina. Deciding to use television for instruction also involves issues of available alternative delivery systems, quality of instructional experience provided by each delivery system, educational goals of the school, and costs. Thus for each question there are many factors that figure into the decision one makes. The one factor that runs through all the decisions is whether, when, how, and how much television content affects children. The material reviewed in this chapter and the preceding one represents what we know about this factor now.

If there were no issues other than television content effects involved in responding to parents' and social commentators' concerns, we could easily say that television content should be controlled and used purposefully to enhance children's well-being. This is because we know that television content *can* lead children to acquire, enhance, and change information, attitudes, and behaviors. We also know that, even if television were *always* used in this way, it would not always affect children, its effects would not always be large, and not all children would ever be affected. When, however, a child in this utopian world was influenced by television content that influence would be a positive one. If there were no extra costs or other trade-offs in using television in this positive way, research certainly indicates that it would be worthwhile.

There are, however, issues other than television content effects involved here. Controlling what is broadcast or watched requires time, effort, some potential loss of freedom of choice, possible restrictions on freedom of expression, and sometimes money. As the costs and trade-offs for control increase, what television content can really contribute to children's development, for good or ill, becomes an important consideration in deciding how much control is worthwhile. Here research fails us. Television content is not the be-all and end-all in children's development and functioning. Its effects in everyday life are occasionally striking, often small, and sometimes nonexistent. On average, they are small. Only some children are affected by any one particular program, series, commercial, or advertising campaign.

We know enough now to specify some, but not all, of the circumstances under which television content will and will not be influential with children. We can use this knowledge to set some upper and lower bounds on what we do. Some content—socially undesirable highly imitatable acts presented in a realistic format, for instance—should be avoided. Other content—neutral acts in any format, for instance—should not be regulated. When broadcasters want to provide programming that will almost certainly contribute to children's well-being, we can tell them a lot about how to do this. Parents should guide children's viewing according to their children's most important needs, interests, and behavioral patterns; for example, keeping prejudiced children away from television content that stereotypes people and guiding scientifically minded children toward the many science, nature, and discovery programs on television. And schools can be assured that, should they choose television as a means of instruction, it will be about as effective as other means and that its effectiveness can be enhanced by attending to the television content, child, and setting variables described earlier.

Yes, we know enough now to set some limits, guidelines, and goals for television content, but there is a gray area where the costs for setting limits, guidelines, and goals have to be weighed against the potential benefits. In this area the balance between costs and benefits will be decided by values. The ethical and philosophical debates required to choose among costs and benefits extend beyond what will ever be known about the transaction between television content and children. Nonetheless, one's understanding of how television content is used by and uses children and of how significant television content can be in children's lives is a crucial element in the debate about how and when to control and guide television content and children's experiences with it.

6

THE MEDIUM AS THE MESSAGE

The television medium affects children not only because it conveys content to them but also because it takes up time in their everyday lives, provides a means for engaging in or avoiding social interaction, and promotes certain information-processing activities and not others.

Earlier, we described four possible roles for television in children's lives: a time-consuming activity, a social (or nonsocial) event, an information-processing task, and an information-providing experience. Chapters 4 and 5 were devoted to understanding television's role as an information-providing experience. The wealth of research about the effects of television content on children was reviewed and conclusions drawn from it. We will now review research about the other three roles ascribed to television. Social scientists, parents, and social commentators alike have been much less concerned about and interested in these television roles. Nonetheless, they represent interesting and potentially important ways in which television also functions in children's lives.

Analyzing television's functions as a time-consuming activity, a social event, or an information-processing task requires taking a somewhat unusual perspective on television. Forget television content. Think instead of television as an option, an environment, a medium. Recognize that when a child watches television—regardless of the content—he or she is spending time that cannot be spent another way, participating in a social environment that often includes other people, and engaging in an information-processing task that has requirements specific to the medium.

TELEVISION AS A TIME-CONSUMING ACTIVITY

Television viewing consumes tremendous amounts of an average American child's time. The best estimates suggest that children three years of age or older commonly spend three or four or even five hours a day watching television. Averages such as these add up to produce startling conclusions. In the summer, when it is easy to play outdoors, preschoolers may spend 40% of their waking hours watching television! By the time youngsters graduate from high school, they may have devoted more time to watching television at home than to attending classes at school! At age 65, average American citizens may have given nine full years of their lives to watching television!

Once the enormity of these figures settles in, most people become very concerned. They worry that the time given to television viewing is time taken away from other important life experiences. They think about the content most children watch most of this time and become even more distressed. They think about how easy and beguiling an activity television viewing is—Hayakawa's sorcerer—and worry still more. Some need go no further to conclude that most children watch far too much television. Even if children gave three to five hours each day to viewing nothing but highly desirable programs, these people contend that it is too much time in one activity, that children need to be involved in a wider range of desirable activities each day.

Some other people want more information before they decide whether most children watch more television than can really contribute positively to their development. They want to know about the viewing patterns of different types of children, about what goes on while children view, about what activities are slighted in order to watch television, and about the effects of giving time to television viewing. With this information, they then feel more confident placing a value on the amount of time children spend watching television at home.

There is little concern about children viewing television in school, because few children ever watch there. At one time, many believed that television would be the panacea our schools cried out for. Master teachers would be available to all children, and infrequent and unusual phenomena and events from the far-flung corners of the world would be brought to every classroom. Today, we find a different reality. About one-third of all teachers have no operative television receiver in their schools, and more than half have no equipment for taping or playback. In a 1980 survey of a large sample of public school teachers, 60% said they never used television in classroom instruction, 20% used it once or twice a semester, 8% once or twice a month, and only 13% at least once a week (National Education Association, 1980). Although a marvelous teaching tool, television is hardly a time-consuming activity at school.

Viewing Patterns

Almost from birth children are exposed to television. Most households have two or more operating sets placed in rooms where family life is conducted. A set in the living room, kitchen, family room, or parents' bedroom is on about seven hours a day. Housework, meals, child care, and conversations go on with television as part of the environment. In these circumstances, it is inevitable that even newborns "watch" some television. Television's auditory signals are always part of the environment those seven hours the set is turned on, and the visual signals are there to view at least some of that time. While parents are washing, feeding, or playing with their babies, they are often also watching television. Sometimes the babies are "watching" too.

Patterns of television viewing change with age. By about two years of age, most children are watching television purposefully. They have a few programs they recognize and like to watch, and they rapidly learn to appreciate the medium so that by about two and a half they behave like seasoned viewers. Older preschoolers watch anywhere from 21 to 35 hours of television each week. Their peak viewing times are early to mid-morning and late afternoon to early evening during the week and early to late morning during the weekend. When children enter school, they adjust their viewing times accordingly. During the early elementary grades, peak viewing times are late afternoon and early to mid-evening during the week and mornings during the weekend. Toward the end of elementary school, weekend morning viewing is declining and viewing is going later into the evening. The total number of hours spent viewing each week does not change much as children progress through elementary school. Most adolescents, however, decrease their viewing as they spend more time participating in afterschool activities, working, and socializing with peers. Their total viewing time averages about 21 hours a week, and their peak viewing times are mid- to late evening.

Viewing patterns also differ according to characteristics other than age. Most variation is in the total amount of time spent viewing rather than in when viewing takes place each day. Of course, children who watch more television altogether must find more time each day to view, but in general their peak viewing times are still the same as those of children their age who view less altogether. So, for instance, adolescent boys and girls have the same peak viewing times even though girls view more than boys. Girls' extra time comes from a secondary peak during the weekday afternoons when they are more likely than boys to be home. When children are compared by social class, those lower in status tend to watch more television than do those higher in status. When they are compared by intelligence, findings differ by age. Among younger children, the more intelligent probably watch a little more, but among older children and adolescents, the less intelligent definitely watch more. When children are compared by ethnic or racial group, few differences have been identified except that black children tend to watch more television than do children of other ethnic backgrounds.

There is one more notable association between characteristics of children and the amount of television they view. It is that less socially well adjusted or satisfied children tend to watch more television than do their better adjusted or more satisfied peers. This is a recurrent finding in studies of younger children, older children, and adolescents. Those children whom others rate as not getting along very well with peers, who are less popular, who spend less time playing with peers, and/or who report being dissatisfied with their peer relationships watch more television.

None of the studies has isolated the causal pattern for the association. Children with less satisfactory peer relationships may watch television simply because other children avoid them and so they have more free time on their hands. Or they may watch so much television that they do not leave enough time to learn to get along with peers. Or they may be less satisfactory companions because they spend more time watching television's bad examples of how to get along with others. Or all three things may account for the association. Or another as yet unidentified variable may cause both amount of viewing and quality of peer relationships. Whatever the cause, those children who have less satisfactory peer relationships spend more time watching television and thereby further remove themselves from opportunities to learn how to get along well with others their own age.

Thus, we see that television viewing consumes several hours of most American children's lives each day. The total amount of viewing time varies somewhat according to children's social class, tested intelligence, racial or ethnic group, gender, and age. Viewing begins in infancy, becomes purposeful in toddlerhood, and continues throughout the rest of life with well documented age-related variations in amount of viewing time. The day-parts during which viewing occurs also change to reflect age-related changes in time required for school, jobs, extracurricular activities, and friendships. There are, then, patterns in children's television viewing, but common to them all is the fact that television viewing is a time-consuming activity for almost all American children for almost all their youth.

The Viewing Activity

The most common image of a child watching television is one of a boy or girl sitting quietly, facing the television set, gazing raptly at the screen for as long as a program is broadcast. Sometimes the image is taken further and the child becomes an enraptured zombie viewer, slack jawed, vacant eyed, and immobilized. Neither image could be less accurate for the majority of children's television viewing time. Indeed, the recent recognition that highly attentive, continuous television viewing is relatively infrequent has left some researchers perplexed about how exactly to measure television viewing.

Most of children's television viewing takes place while other things are going on. Eating meals and snacking are very common. So too are playing with toys and doing homework. When possible, household chores are also done with the television set going. And, of course, children talk to and otherwise interact with other people while they are watching television. Sometimes the conversation centers on the television program or ideas stimulated by it, but very often the conversation is entirely unrelated to television. And, as we will see more in the section "Television as a Social Event," there may be some snuggling, rough-housing, or fighting going on during viewing. Our best estimates suggest that more than half of children's television viewing time involves television and one or more of these many other household activities.

What television viewing time is really like is well illustrated by the following summary of a mother's observation of her six-year-old son watching television on a typical Saturday morning in a middle-class household in a city on the West Coast. The mother had been trained to observe carefully and record events on a special form, because she and her child were participating in a research project.

> At 8:00 a.m. the opening credits begin. The child is in the living room and asks his mother, who is trying to be unobtrusive yet normally interactive, "Did this just come on, Mom?" She answers, "Yes." At 8:02 the cartoon story begins. At 8:13 a short activity segment is shown. The boy watches both. At 8:14 commercials begin, and the boy tells his mother that Lando Calrissian is the only action figure that does not come with the Cloud City set. At 8:15 another activity segment is watched. At 8:16 another cartoon story begins. A younger sister enters the room and is told to leave because "I'm watching this

show." At 8:21 commercials begin and the boy leaves the room to get something to eat. He remains out of the room, but probably within hearing range, while the second part of the cartoon story, three activity segments, and commercials are broadcast. He re-enters the room at 8:30 while a public service announcement (PSA) about sports is being broadcast. He quietly watches another PSA, the station break, and more commercials. At 8:33 another cartoon story begins. While the youngster watches it, he bounces and jumps up and down, exclaiming "rock concert," and finally asks how much longer the show will go on. At 8:44 he laughs at another activity segment and says "That's enough TV for me." He watches another minute of commercials and then leaves the room at 8:49, three minutes after another cartoon story begins. He return at 8:55 to watch an activity segment about physical fitness. During the ensuing seven minutes of commercials, news, station identification, and PSAs he tells his mother about advertised toys he wants, sings along with a commercial, talks with his mother about making things from construction paper, and voices approval of the message in a PSA. Beginning at 9:02 he watches a short cartoon story and two activity segments. At 9:11, three minutes into the next cartoon story, he goes out and gets a toy that he plays with while "watching" television. Soon after that he goes to his room to listen to records.

Children's television viewing can be a very discontinuous experience, not only because programs are interrupted by commercial and noncommerical content but also because viewing is interrupted by other life activities. The few estimates we have of actual viewing at home suggest that somewhere around 40% of all programs children (or their parents) say they watch are actually watched from beginning to end with only minor interruptions for other activities. The rest of the programs are not really watched in their entirety, even though children and their parents feel that enough has been watched to report that children had viewed the programs.

Fine-grained analyses of children's viewing behaviors suggest that, even when children are attentive viewers, they do not look at the screen continuously. Whether viewing with peers, with family members, or alone, children look away from the screen often. Until youngsters are about two and a half years old they do not pay much attention to television except when confined to a small space with only the set for entertainment. Around two and a half there is a dramatic increase in attention to the set; children become viewers. Still, preschoolers look at and look away from the set frequently during viewing. Some studies suggest an average of 150 looks at and away from *Sesame Street* during an hour's viewing, with most looks averaging less than 15 seconds in length. Work with older children and even college students also suggests that attentive viewers look away from the screen often, although it is believed that looks at the screen tend to increase in length as children mature.

Looking at the screen and away from it are naturally prompted by events in the viewing environment, but they are also apparently guided by what is being broadcast. If children are watching the screen, all other things being equal they tend to look away when commercials come on, when content becomes boring, or when messages are hard to understand. If children are not watching the screen they tend to look back when there is a change in the audio track indicating a change in content, when there is an unusual sound that would ordinarily attract attention in everyday life (e.g., screams, crashes, sirens, cries), or when the audio track is such that children decide the content will be understandable to them. These characterizations of children's viewing behaviors are based primarily on studies of young children, but the few data we have on older children suggest that their viewing is similarly discontinuous and purposive.

Television viewing behavior can be examined with even finer-grained analyses in which eye movements are charted. From them we can learn exactly what parts of the visual images on the screen are being examined at any moment. Eye movement research shows that children do not always look at all parts of the screen or even at all parts crucial to understanding the message the program creators intended to convey. As we saw in the discussion in Chapters 2 and 3 of how children make sense of television content, both children and content can contribute to determining what is looked at. As children develop, they become more able to pick out important content and look at it more than or instead of unimportant content. Children also pick out and look more at content that they themselves find worthwhile; for instance, when male and female characters are both attractive and important to a story, boys and girls will each tend to look more at same-sex rather than opposite-sex characters. And, naturally enough, visual displays and changes in them can be orchestrated so as to lead the eye to the important content or to distract it from that content. Whether the primary cause rests in the child viewer or in the content viewed, however, the result is that children's viewing of the television screen itself is not an activity in which relevant content is continuously attended to.

From toddlers to adolescents, then, child viewers are neither unmoving sponges nor stuporous zombies. Home viewing, more often than not, is a discontinuous activity that includes leaving the room in which the television set is operating, doing other things while viewing, looking away from the screen often, and looking at parts of the screen that are not very important for conveying the message. At times, television content is truly an irrelevant background in the child's environment. At other times, it is truly the main event even if the child's watching includes periods of listening but not watching and periods of neither watching nor listening. During these times children are apparently actively processing television content and guiding their television viewing activities accordingly.

Sources of Viewing Time

Given that children are spending three or more hours a day watching television, one wonders where they find all that time. Some activities that engaged children a generation or two ago must occur infrequently or never for today's television-viewing children. And those children who now watch five hours of television daily must arrange their lives a little differently than do those children who only watch three hours daily. By looking at the kinds of activities television viewing displaces or replaces, we can learn something about the functions of television in children's lives, get leads as to the effects of giving time to television viewing, and begin to place a value on the time given to television viewing.

Three strategies have been used to identify activities that are displaced or replaced by television viewing. Two can only be used when television is being introduced into a culture. First, one can compare people's activities in similar communities with and without television, and, second, one can compare activities of people before and after they have access to television (see Cramond, 1976, and Murray, 1980, for reviews of such studies). In the 1950s and early 1960s, when television was being adopted by Westernized countries, Hilde Himmelweit and her colleagues in England (Himmelweit et al., 1958) and Wilbur Schramm and his colleagues in the United States (Schramm et al., 1961) conducted classic studies using these strategies. Today, most countries have television and so one can resort to these strategies only for people living in remote areas or in developing countries just now getting television reception. Alternatively, one can turn to the third strategy, that of comparing the activities of heavy and light viewers or of viewers and nonviewers in countries and communities where television access is universal.

All three strategies are obviously fraught with interpretive perils. When comparing communities with and without television, it is hard to be certain that they are similar but for television. Isn't the town getting television first likely to be less geographically isolated, to have a more modern and innovative spirit, or to have more buying power among its residents? When comparing families before and after the introduction of television, it is hard to be certain that other important features of their lives do not also change during this period. While television is joining the family, might not an older child grow into a teenager, a close neighbor family move away, or high unemployment hit the community? When comparing heavy and light viewers or viewers and nonviewers, isn't it likely that factors that led them to their viewing status (e.g., a religion that discourages television viewing, an elitist disdain for television, or living in an environment in which it is dangerous to go outside the home) would account for findings as well as would amount of television viewed?

As was true for the better nonexperimental studies of television content effects, the better studies of time use have made every effort to rule out alternative explanations for differences they wish to attribute to the presence of television. They cannot resort to experimentation to rule out alternative explanations and clarify causal relationships. We, however, can look at the quality of the nonexperimental work and use the best of it to learn where children find the time for watching television.

The largest identifiable chunk of time given up in order to watch television came from other entertainment-oriented mediated experiences. Once televisions came into their homes, children spent much less time listening to radio dramas and comedies than they had previously. They also chose television over movies, reducing their attendance at theaters from one or more times a week to barely once a month. In addition, children made several small adjustments in what had always been their relatively low level of involvement in other media. They read fewer comics. They looked at general circulation magazines less. They decreased book reading a little, more the reading of light fiction than of other kinds of literature. In short, children found time for television viewing by giving up time they had previously spent with other mediated, entertainment experiences.

Children also made small adjustments in other daily activities. They slept about a quarter of an hour less each night. They spent about ten or fifteen minutes less on homework each day. They decreased by about half an hour each week the time spent in unstructured outdoor play with peers. They did not decrease their involvement in formal organizations, household chores, extracurricular school activities, or school. And they actually increased their time spent with other family members, again by not more than about a quarter of an hour each day.

All in all, time use studies suggest that the introduction of television brought few major and many minor changes to the fabric of children's daily lives. These studies do not, however, show us where all the time children now spend watching television actually came from. No one yet has been able to identify three or five or seven hours of daily activities that are given up in order to watch television for that amount of time. Part of the explanation for this failure probably lies in the fact that many children do other things while they watch television. Much of what might once have been time devoted solely to eating breakfast, for instance, is now time given both to watching television and to eating breakfast. If so, today's children are living in "noisier" environments and time-sharing more activities than did previous generations of children, and heavier viewers are doing so more than light viewers.

Most often in thinking about how children's daily lives change to accommodate television viewing one imagines simple trade-offs of time. To get three hours of television viewing time each day a child in this model gives up three hours of other activities that fulfill the same functions and provide the same gratifications for the child. The three-hour daily quota is made up of an hour of daily radio listening, 20 minutes from the Saturday movie, 10 minutes a day of hanging out with friends, 20 minutes a day of reading comics and pulp fiction, and who knows what other idle pastimes. Nothing has shifted except where a child finds his or her light entertainment. This model certainly has some merit to it. It represents part of reality, but only part.

A more accurate model of how life patterns are adjusted to accommodate television viewing involves many small trade-offs in activities, increases in time sharing, and changes in the functions of activities. In order to watch television, children give up some activities that we regard as similar light entertainment. They also, however, give up some time that otherwise would be given to activities that fulfill different functions (e.g., doing homework), and they even do more of a few things (e.g., family conversation). Moreover, children reorganize activities and their functions rather than simply displacing activities functionally similar to television viewing. Thus, in order to watch television children make many, mostly small adjustments in their other activities and somewhat reorganize the functions various activities fulfill for them. This is a picture of controlled complex adaptation not one of radical change or simple substitution.

Effects of Giving Time to Viewing

Many parents, teachers, social commentators, and social scientists believe that children spend too much time watching television. They often assume that time taken away from televison viewing would then be given to activities that are better for children. If children were not gazing at television, they would be reading, doing homework, cleaning their rooms, pursuing hobbies, playing with friends or siblings, or sleeping, or so the argument goes. The time use data reviewed in the preceding section hardly suggest, however, that the majority of television viewing time is time taken away from these other laudable pursuits.

Some people recognize that children would not be continuously engaged in more wholesome activities were it not for television, yet they still believe that children would be better off watching less television. They argue that even squabbling with a sibling, daydreaming, and pestering parents to provide entertainment are sometimes better learning experiences for children than is television viewing. They realize that out of all experiences children should have, television viewing provides only certain kinds, mostly the opportunity to process lifelike audiovisual stimuli that are well organized but not responsive to the individual viewer. Depending on the value they place on the kinds of experiences television provides, these people worry either that children watch any television at all or that children watch too much television.

Several deficits are thought to accrue to children who watch too much television. It is easy to imagine them if one just thinks of what television viewing does and does not entail. Since television viewing is not interactive and not contingent on children's at-home behaviors, children who watch a lot of television should not be highly skilled in social interactions. Since television viewing involves little if any talking, creating of visual images, or directing of one's activities, children who watch a lot of television should be rather inarticulate, uncreative, and passive. Since television viewing involves few of the skills required for reading and takes time away from reading and doing homework, children who watch a lot of television should not do so well in school. These are the main deficiencies ascribed to overdoses of television viewing, but a thoughtful person can certainly construct several other unpalatable outcomes.

There have been empirical assessments of the accuracy of some of these claims. As reported in the section "Viewing Patterns," those children who watch more television are also likely to have less satisfactory peer relationships. Due to the methods used to uncover this relationship, we cannot know whether socially under-skilled children choose to watch more television or children who watch more television develop deficits in their social skills. However, the relationship at least does not contradict the assumption that too much television viewing can lead to deficits in social interaction skills. In contrast, the little evidence we have about the relationships between television viewing and verbal skills, creativity, and activity provides scant support for the hypothesized negative effects.

Of all predictions about the effects of giving time to television viewing, probably the best tested and most strongly supported is that children who watch more television do less well in school. Most often reading achievement is the area of academic performance investigated, but achievement in other academic areas has also been examined. The simplest reported finding is that the more television children watch the less well they do in reading and other school subjects.

Some studies have identified a rather more complicated curvilinear relationship for lower class children. For them, more time given to television viewing each day, up to a maximum of about two hours, tends to be associated with better academic performance. More viewing than that leads to decreased performance. A plausible explanation for this finding rests on understanding what academically relevant experiences television and lower class environments *on the average* can provide. For some children, run-of-the-mill entertainment television can add some academically relevant experiences to their lives, for example, grammatical standard English and well-structured narratives. In small doses, television can enrich these children's lives. In larger doses it takes time away from more academically relevant experiences they would otherwise have.

The effects, then, of giving time to television viewing are, like the effects of television content, less strong and less horrible than the worst imagined, less good than the best imagined, and more evident than those who pooh-pooh concern about television would like. Television viewing undeniably consumes many hours of almost every child's week. At least some of these hours would otherwise be given to more socially valued activities or to activities such as squabbling that require some socially useful skills. Some of the hours come from adding television viewing to other ongoing activities. The consequences of giving many hours to television viewing are as yet not well documented, but there is reason to believe that with more television viewing time comes less skill in social interactions and decreased performance in school. And without a doubt, with more televison viewing time comes less time in other activities and more time with time-shared activities.

TELEVISION AS A SOCIAL EVENT

Television viewing is an event that can encourage or discourage social interaction. A child—or any family member for that matter—can use television to avoid social interaction by retreating to a place where it is possible to watch alone or by becoming absorbed enough in television to shut other people out or by requiring other people to be quiet so that the program can be enjoyed. Alternatively, television viewing can be a shared activity in which the child and other family members find the opportunity to talk, to sit close, to fight, or to be quietly companionable. Even when television viewing is not going on, television can be a stimulus to social interaction. All parents sometimes engage their children in interactions designed to guide or control the children's use of television, and parents, siblings, other family members, and peers all sometimes use television content as something to talk about or to guide play. Whether with family or with peers, then, television operates as a potential social event for children irrespective of its content.

Family Interactions

In thinking about television as an opportunity for family interaction, one needs to recognize that television viewing provides a setting in which family members can interact or not as they choose, operates as an activity over which parents may wish to exert some control, and offers topics for conversations among family members. Interview and questionnaire studies with children, parents, and families have provided basic information about how television functions in these roles. A richer view requires an anthropological approach that is rarely adopted by researchers in communication, education, and psychology. Fortunately, a few hardy souls such as James Lull and Daniel Anderson have recently ventured into children's homes and stayed awhile.

At home, children view with other family members slightly less than half of all their viewing hours. While viewing, they may engage in many other social interactions. The description of a six-year-old boy's Saturday morning viewing (see "The Viewing Activity" section) illustrates that during viewing the boy also talked several times with his mother about topics stimulated by what he saw on television and once gave his sister orders about not watching television with him. There are also interactions during television viewing that are essentially unrelated either to the act of viewing or the content viewed. In interviews, about three-quarters of elementary and secondary school age children confirm that they sometimes or quite often talk to family members while watching television. Only about a quarter of the students say the conversations are only about television.

The communications researcher James Lull (1980) has proposed a typology for the social uses of television, based on his ethnographic data on the behavior of over 200 families in their own homes and on the uses and gratifications literature. He proposes two major types of social uses of television: structural and relational. When it is used in structural ways, television provides reassuring background noise and companionship (environmental use) and a means for marking time and organizing activity (regulative use). When it is used in relational ways, television provides subject matter for conversation (communication facilitation), opportunities for physical and emotional contact (affiliation/avoidance), potentially useful examples of interpersonal interactions (social learning), and opportunities to enact roles and power relationships (competence/dominance). Whether or not this typology is entirely correct, it nicely illustrates the range of social interactions that the television viewing event permits.

Television viewing also engenders family interactions, because it is one children's activity over which parents and other family members want to exercise some control. Family members care some about how much television children view, when they view, what must be done before viewing, where they view, with whom they view, and what they view. We should not over-emphasize the frequency of family interactions about these matters, however, as most children and parents report that only a modicum of control is exercised over children's viewing. The areas that provoke the greatest parental efforts at control are those of what is watched, what must be done before viewing, and when viewing will occur. In addition, many parents take away television viewing privileges as a means of punishing children's infractions in other areas of their lives. Thus, television viewing is an occasion for a social event not only because people view together but also because people want to regulate children's television viewing behaviors.

Children also find that television viewing provides content for conversations with parents and other family members, conversations that occur during or after viewing. The reported increase in time spent in conversation with family members after the introduction of television into a household or community (see "Sources of Viewing Time") is usually ascribed to conversations during television viewing about what is being viewed. The earlier description of the six-year-old boy's television viewing shows him talking with his mother about the products being advertised, the broadcast schedule, the PSAs, and the cartoon stories. In one interview study, slightly more than 50% of a sample of sixth graders reported sometimes or often talking about television with their parents, while about 30% of tenth grade boys and 60% of tenth grade girls also reported that such conversations occurred fairly often (Lyle & Hoffman, 1972a).

All children, then, find that television viewing provides opportunities for family interactions that take place before, during, and after viewing. Frequently, too, several kinds of social events—conversation about television content, interaction aimed at regulating viewing, and social interchange in the context of viewing—occur together, making television viewing a very social event among family members.

Peer Interactions

By all accounts, most of children's television viewing is at home, alone or with other family members. Children infrequently use television viewing itself as a social event with peers, but what can be seen and what has been seen on television are frequently the bases for peer interactions. Often, they are topics of conversations: "Have you seen the new show about a $3 million motorcycle?" or "Did you watch *Roots* last night and see how they used to sell slaves?" Sometimes they are the blueprints for play: "Let's play *Superfriends* and I'll be Batman!" or "Let's pretend I'm King Friday and you're Prince Tuesday."

Children report that they often talk with friends about television programs. In one study (Lyle & Hoffman, 1972a), for instance, sixth grade children reported that television was the second most frequent topic of conversation with their friends. Among tenth graders, it was the third most frequent topic for boys and the sixth for girls. Informal observations of young children and their friends in school and at play suggest such conversations about television begin at a very young age. Some theorists have even speculated that television, by providing a common ground for conversation, helps maintain social cohesion among peers.

Children also use televison programs as rough blueprints for play. At one time children in my neighborhood played games based on Saturday morning cartoons and prime-time crime dramas. In

Planet of the Apes, one group of boys and girls led by one or two boys took the roles of the apes and captured, enslaved, and generally mistreated another group of children who took the roles of the humans. In *Charlie's Angels,* three older girls took the roles of the crime-stopping angels and chased, captured, and punished the other children, mostly boys, who took the roles of the criminals. More formal data obtained from interviews with children and observations of them in schools and on playgrounds suggest that popular television programs provide roles and action sequences for younger children's play and specific phrases, gestures, dress styles, and actions for older children's and adolescents' interactions.

Significance of Socializing with Television

Television is securely woven into the social fabric of children's lives. About this we are sure, but we know little about its significance. Consider the unanswered questions just about television as a topic of conversation: Is television content a strong stimulus to conversation? Does television give children more to talk about than do other experiences they have? Do children who watch more television have more to talk about? Does talking about television give children more or better friendships or stronger or happier relationships with family members? We know that children talk with family members and friends about television, but we know little more than that. There is no way now, other than logical argumentation, to begin to place value on television as a social event. This should not deter us, however, from appreciating the several ways in which children can put television to use in the service of their social relationships with family members and peers.

TELEVISION AS AN INFORMATION-PROCESSING TASK

About 20 years ago Marshall McLuhan (1964) reminded us that television is a medium as well as messages. What does this mean? It surely does not mean, as Fred Allen once quipped, that television is a medium because nothing in it is ever well done. No, instead it means that television has characteristics that transcend its content and define it regardless of content. Social scientists and educators have recently become interested in identifying these characteristics of the television medium, elucidating the information-processing task it presents to viewers, and understanding the significance to child viewers of spending hours engaged in this particular information-processing environment.

The Medium

For researchers, theorists, and aestheticians, television is a medium at several different levels. It is a technology that can deliver certain signals in certain ways. It is a means of communication with established types of content and aesthetic standards. It is a set of codes that creators and viewers alike use to construct and convey experiences. Some characteristics of the medium are necessary concomitants of the technology itself, but many more are conventions and conveniences that we have established to make the medium useful and to bring it under social control. At the beginning of the book several of these characteristics were introduced in order to illustrate the task that children undertake when they construct meaning from television stimuli. Here we will fill out the picture of what this medium is like regardless of its content.

As a technology, television has certain defining characteristics. It provides auditory and visual signals, but it provides no tactile, olefactory, or spatial signals. The auditory and visual signals are both capable of changing on their own over time without any effort by the viewer. The auditory signal comes through a system that restricts the frequency range within which the sounds can vary and localizes the source of sound to one place. The visual signal is a series of dots that are transmitted line by ever-changing line. McLuhan was most struck by this aspect of the television medium, emphasizing the integrative work the viewer must do to create an image out of all those dots.

Another important technological characteristic of the television medium is the amount of control the child has over what is being viewed. Commercial, public, and pay over-the-air broadcasting, narrowcasting, satellite transmission, and cable all share the same characteristic of allowing the child no more control over what is viewed than turning the on/off switch and selecting a channel. Once a channel has been chosen, the child must cope with television's auditory and visual signals as they are transmitted at a pace and in an order that the producers determined and the child cannot change. Videotape and videodisc players, on the other hand, allow the child to select one of two or three paces, to stop to look at one image, and to alter the order in which content is viewed. Videotape and videodisc players are, however, available to only a small minority of children, and even for these children most viewing time is devoted to over-the-air broadcasting and cable. For these reasons, uninterruptibility, nonrepeatability, and uncontrollability are characteristics of the television medium most children use most of the time.

While the technology itself determines some characteristics of the medium, many more have simply been chosen to be "standard operating procedure" by those who use television as a means of communication. Of the many kinds of auditory and visual signals the technology can convey, by convention we restrict television signals primarily to speech, with some sounds from everyday life and a little music, laughter, and applause thrown in, and to human, animal, and object behavior through space and time. Television is not the medium of choice for conveying print, drawings, still photographs, paintings, mathematical formulas, musical scores, symphonies, or operas. To be sure, each can be found on television, but they are not what is characteristic of the medium. Some are eschewed because the technology does not permit them to be done really well; for instance, music suffers when its full range and power are cut down by the television signal and speakers we have now. Others are eschewed because the technology permits more; for instance, lifelike images, movement, and combined audio-video signals are so easy with television that one chooses them over arbitrary codes, static images, audio signals only, or video signals only.

Over the years we have further delimited how the television medium is used as a means of communication. Most often it is a storyteller—even when it is telling about news, public affairs, or products. Most often it is entertaining. Even instructional television programs these days are supposed to be enjoyable, lighthearted, dramatic, and engaging. Most often it is technically well done. Those who produce, broadcast, and view television expect its content to be conveyed with sharp images, clean cuts, special effects, clear speech, and a variety of camera angles. It is not necessary for the television medium to be an entertaining, technically sophisticated storyteller that uses changing everyday sounds and images to unfold a story. Yet these characteristics are so much a part of television that most children accept them as part of the medium itself.

Children also accept as part of the medium the specific codes that are used to convey television's content. Some codes are the same as those for everyday life: All the linguistic and paralinguistic codes that operate in face-to-face conversation operate in conversations on television, and all the nonverbal codes that operate in everyday life operate in settings, actions, and interactions on television. Other codes are different from those for everyday life: There are codes for what content is presented and what left out, for music, for camera work, for editing, and for special effects. This is not the place to describe these codes in great detail (see Huston & Wright, 1983, and Salomon, 1979, for more discussion), but it is worth a few lines to illustrate how they work:

> A long shot shows a woman looking out from a window in the upper right part of a 10-story brick apartment building; the camera zooms in to her face; a long shot shows girls playing with Barbie dolls in the street below and the audio track carries sounds of rushing cars, screeching brakes, and heavy metal music; the scene fades out; a new scene fades in over it; in slow motion girls are playing in the same street with rag dolls and clothespin dolls and the audio track carries sounds of slow trotting horses and lullaby-like music; slowly the camera moves closer to and then over the scene and comes to rest on one girl's face; the girl's face seems like a younger version of the woman's face.

It is easy to see in the illustration how many codes are used to create a mood, tell a story, or present information on television. These codes are always used for all types of television content. They are not altogether required by the technology itself, but over years of use they have come to constitute an inextricable part of the television medium.

No one yet has devised a system for categorizing media that encompasses all the types of medium characteristics we have described, but two systems have received some attention in communications, education, and psychology. McLuhan's (1964) system was the first. He divided media according to how much work the user had to do to construct a complete internal stimulus using the medium's signals. Hot media are those whose signals are complete, who present sensory stimuli filled with data and therefore require little or no work from the child to complete them. Cool media are those whose signals are incomplete, who present sensory stimuli that are not well filled with data and therefore require participation from the child to complete the sensory image. The viewer's need to integrate television's lines of dots in order to form a complete image made television a cool medium in McLuhan's system. Other cool media include the telephone, cartoons, speech, and hieroglyphic characters. Hot media include radio, film, photography, print, and the phonetic alphabet. McLuhan's system is clearly based on an analysis of the physical stimuli media transmit and of the information-processing activities they therefore require of users seeking to encode their content.

Gavriel Salomon (1979), U.S.-trained Israeli educator and researcher, has proposed an analysis that focuses on the symbol systems used by media. He argues that media are complex entities composed of a technology, contents, situations of use, and symbol systems. The symbol systems ordinarily used by a medium are seen, however, as the most important attribute, for they give each medium its essential character or mode of representation and they are the means by which all medium-based cognition and learning occurs.

Based largely on the work of Goodman (1968), Salomon suggests that symbol systems, which are composed of symbols and rules for combining them, are best characterized by the relationship between the symbol system and the field of reference it represents. Some systems involve discrete, discontinuous symbols and combinations of symbols that have a one-to-one correspondence to similarly discrete, discontinuous elements and patterns in the field of reference. Music and mathematics are good examples of these systems. Each note on a sheet of music corresponds to one and only one sound from a musical instrument, and each plus and minus sign corresponds to one and only one operation with numbers. At the other end are systems, like pictures and contour maps, with continuous elements referring to continuous fields or at least to fields that are not easily broken into bits. Symbol systems of the first type are called notational, and those of the second type, nonnotational. In between these two types are mixed symbol systems. Salomon's formulation is clearly based on an analysis of media codes, those characteristics that come by the convention of usage to be associated with each technology.

In addition to these two systems for characterizing media, several researchers have selected a subset of the characteristics of the television medium and sought to systematize them (e.g., Anderson & Lorch, 1983; Huston & Wright, 1983; Krull, 1983; Watt & Welch, 1983). All involve examining television in ways that relate more to *how* content is conveyed than to *what* content is conveyed. To the extent that such a differentiation can be made, they focus on the form of television and not on its content.

Foremost is the work of the psychologists Aletha Huston and John Wright, and of their students, who have codified the "formal features" of television and explored their implications for children's attention to, understanding of, and learning from television. Early in their program of research they developed a summary taxonomy of the formal features of television programs. At the macro level they identified action, visual pace, auditory pace, and variability. The micro level they divided into visual and auditory elements, many of which are used by producers to create the macro level formal features. Visual micro level features include cuts, pans and trucks, zooms, fades and dissolves, and special effects. Audio microlevel features include dialogue, nonhuman vocalizations, music, sound effects, laugh tracks, and narration. Having established a working taxonomy, Huston and Wright proceeded to demonstrate that short cartoons, long cartoons, and live action children's programs differ in many of these formal features even though all are aimed at children of about the same age.

Other systems for characterizing the television medium have examined overall program complexity, the complexity of static and dynamic auditory and visual features, the age and sex of audio track voices and visual people, the rate of change of stimuli, and the like. All these systems focus on the codes of television, the symbol systems that society has somewhat arbitrarily established for the medium, construct partial grammars for them, and explore the consequences for children of variations in how these codes are used. No system encompasses all aspects of television's form, but each illuminates and organizes a portion of the many elements used by producers to make programs and by children to construct meaning for programs.

Thus, from several different perspectives, television is a medium that presents certain information-processing tasks to children. It offers stimuli for some senses and not others. It usually presents stimuli at its own pace, without allowing the child viewer to choose repetitions, interruptions, changes in order, or changes in pace. It emphasizes certain content and aesthetic standards over others. It uses some symbol systems and not others. It has formal features that can be deliberately manipulated by television producers. Together these characteristics describe a medium that, regardless of the content being presented, offers certain information-processing tasks and opportunities to children. What impact these tasks and opportunities have on viewers is a question of some interest these days.

Effects of Processing Television

As a medium, or information-processing task, television has the opportunity to engage children in certain experiences that should influence their development. The author Gore Vidal described these influences in a newspaper interview in which he was critical of younger writers. After noting that "the TV babies are now writing books," he went on to complain, "They have very short attention spans. The scenes are very, very short. The dialogue is very, very short. There's a lot of jumping around. You get the sense of somebody shifting channels all the time" (Gore Vidal, 1984, p. 10).

Consider the three types of medium characteristics described in the preceding section and what they might mean for children's development: (1) Television signals come to children at a predetermined pace over which they have no control, and so viewing could lead children to become adept at picking out important information from an ongoing flow of stimulation; (2) Most television programs use a storytelling or narrative mode, and so viewing could lead children to prefer that all their learning come from hearing stories in which the instructional information is embedded; and (3) Television usually presents close-ups of the faces of those who are speaking, just as though the intended receivers were looking at the speakers' faces, and so viewing could lead children to attend to speakers' faces rather than their hands, some other body part, or objects in the environment. We will now explore such effects of television as an information-processing task, organizing the discussion by type of medium characteristic.

Let us begin with comparisons of different media (see Olson, 1974, for a fine compilation of articles on media characteristics and effects). The assumption here is that fundamental, probably technologically based, differences in media produce related differences in outcomes for those using them. Some social scientists (e.g., Clark, 1983; Olson & Bruner, 1974; Schramm, 1977) argue that these differences are only in the information-processing skills cultivated and not at all in the content learned. For example, from reading about dinosaurs in a book children learn about dinosaurs and about reading, while from watching a television program about dinosaurs children learn about dinosaurs and about watching television. To support this position they aggregate results from a multitude of studies, mostly in education, showing little if any difference in academic achievement or content learning when the same content is delivered by different media. They then argue that the important issue in choosing media for children in and out of school is what information-processing skills one wants children to develop, not what content one wants them to learn.

Other researchers, still comparing different media, have suggested that more or less technologically based medium differences can also produce different knowledge outcomes, at least when the knowledge would be derived from different information-processing activities. For example, most television presentations concretize content so that even very abstract concepts such as liberty and justice are depicted explicitly, while print presentations of abstract concepts are not as often concrete. One might expect, then, that children viewing a television program about liberty would learn more concrete visual representations for liberty—the flag, the

Statue of Liberty, or voting, while children reading about liberty would have more verbal analogies for it. Exploring this question requires a very microscopic approach. Gross comparisons of mathematics or science learning from television and other media are unlikely to show the kinds of subtle medium-based differences predicted here.

Laurene Meringoff (1980), in her dissertation research, was one of the first to provide empirical evidence for medium-based differences in knowldege that had to be tied to the information-processing activities required by different media. She compared story knowledge when elementary school age children were read to from an illustrated African folktale and when they saw a television program with the book's illustrations animated and the book reader providing the narration. Despite the very great similarity between the two presentations, television and the picture book had somewhat different effects on children's learning. Children who watched television included more actions and gestured more in retelling the story, and they relied on visual content in making inferences about implicit events in the story. Children who were read the story recalled more figurative language and based their inferences more on the words of the story and information from outside the story. These results clearly show that "the same story" becomes subtly altered according to the medium by which it is conveyed and that these alterations affect what children learn and what skills they use.

Since the original study, Meringoff, her colleagues, and other researchers have conducted several similar cross-media studies. Some have made the two media presentations even more similar (e.g., an audio tape for a radio condition and the same audio tape as the soundtrack for a television condition) and have usually then found fewer outcome differences. Others have reported medium differences in the extent to which creative alternative endings were suggested for a story. Still others have confirmed that different media presentations of the same story result both in no differences in central content learned and in many differences in details and nuances learned and in inferences made.

Results from several different studies and researchers do not add up to an unambiguous picture of how media differ in their effects on children. In general, they confirm that the major messages of a presentation are equally well learned when they are conveyed by different media but that specific details of knowledge, specific ways of drawing upon prior knowledge to understand the presentation, and some specific uses of messages may vary according to medium.

At the least, work to date supports the propositions that different media, because of their technological characteristics, present different learning opportunities to children, that these opportunities relate to the information-processing activities in which children engage while using each medium, and that these information-processing activities relate to children's subsequent knowledge and skills.

If technological differences in media lead to different outcomes in users, then it is not unreasonable to expect that differences in the content and aesthetics typically conveyed could also affect children. Television's entertaining, high quality, highly visual, storytelling characteristics have led some to suggest that it leads children to decide that television is an easy medium to use, to expect all information-processing tasks to be as easy and sugar-coated, and to adopt television norms for any audiovisual productions children themselves make.

Soon after television became popular, teachers began to complain that children expected to be entertained in school too and did not want to make any effort to process more demanding material. A few teachers still worry, but many have forgotten what pretelevision children were like and many more themselves grew up with television. Earlier, we reviewed evidence that children who watch more television often do less well in reading and other school subjects. This was attributed to the amount of time children gave to television viewing rather than to reading at home, but another possible cause would be that television has led children to expect easy, entertaining information-processing tasks not demanding tasks like reading.

Recently, Salomon (1983) has returned to some of these ideas and formalized them. He argues that, because children think of television as an easy medium from which to process information, they invest little mental energy (AIME) in it. As a consequence, children learn less from television than they otherwise could. Salomon and others have shown that children do indeed perceive television to be easier to use than some other media, especially print. In recent work Salomon (1984) has also shown that sixth graders report investing more effort in reading a narrative story than in watching it on a video monitor, make more correct inferences for the print version, and for both the print and television versions make more correct inferences the more effort they report investing. None of the predicted effects occurred, however, for recognition of central content in either the print or video version. Others, too, have failed to find much evidence that AIME predicts much about learning main content from television.

If the television medium cultivates children's preferences for easy, entertaining experiences, it also apparently establishes aesthetic norms for them. Teachers who have asked students to produce their own programs or commercials find that children have well-developed images of better and worse television, images based entirely on their home viewing. Even Navajo youth living on a reservation are not immune to television's style setting (Worth & Adair, 1972). When given the opportunity to make films, these youth began with an aesthetic and storytelling style that clearly derived from their Navajo language and culture. The film teachers found their films charming, but the film makers found them inferior approximations to the ideal. With each successive try the Navajo youth came closer to producing films like what they saw on television, thereby demonstrating the medium's power to influence norms and expectations for how messages are communicated.

The codes that the television medium uses to communicate its messages may also have effects on children. As we learned earlier, variations in codes can guide children's attention away from and to the television screen. And, certainly, understanding the codes increases the likelihood that children will understand television content as the producer intended. If you think back to the earlier example of a woman looking into the street and remembering her own childhood, you can easily recognize how knowing the possible meanings for cuts and slow motion would help a child understand that sequence as the producer intended it to be understood. The best producers deliberately use codes in this way to help convey the content and feeling they want.

These same codes can also be used to cultivate certain information-processing patterns or skills. Camera work, cutting, and zooms in and out, for example, can be combined to guide children's visual processing of television images. Children can thereby be taught visual search strategies, how to look at paintings, how to compare figures for similarities and differences, and where to look when people are talking in sign language. Research on preschool and kindergarten children's learning of such information-processing skills from *Sesame Street* has unambiguously demonstrated that the medium's codes can be used to such educational advantage. Salomon (1979), too, has demonstrated some of these possibilities in two studies with older children. In one, the ability of the camera to zoom in on detail was used to teach children this visual inspection strategy, while quick cuts from a long shot to a detail were used to give other children practice in the same strategy. Most television programs, however, are not designed to teach any particular information-processing patterns or skills, and there is no evidence so far that everyday television viewing has any effects on children's information-processing abilities.

A final use of television codes is to help create certain feeling states in child viewers. As Huston, Wright, and their students have so compellingly demonstrated, variations in codes are routinely associated with variations in feeling tone. Commercials for girls' toys are softer and use fewer cuts, more fades, and softer music, while commercials for boys' toys are harder and use more cuts, fewer fades, and louder music with a more driving rhythm (Huston, Greer, Wright, Welch, & Ross, 1984). Such variations ought to influence viewers' feelings, but the evidence is mixed. One study, for example, found that children who viewed *Sesame Street*, a program that uses variations in codes to create fast-paced, ever-changing content, felt no more agitated and in need of action than did other children (Anderson, Levin, & Lorch, 1977).

The concept of formal features has sometimes been criticized because form and content cannot be independent when it comes to conveying moods and feelings. We rarely find, for example, that harsh, aggressive, fast-paced action is conveyed with few cuts, many close-ups, slow camera movement, and fades rather than cuts, nor is dreamy, romantic, nostalgic, or sad content conveyed with many cuts, rapid camera movement, and sharp lighting. The magnitude of formal features' contributions to viewers' feelings and activity levels should not be exaggerated and their relationships to content should be acknowledged. Nonetheless, their contribution to creating and modulating feelings connected to content cannot be denied.

There are, then, many reasons to believe that the characteristics of the television medium as an information-processing task can be important for children. Comparing its characteristics to those of other media suggests that in viewing television children engage in some information-processing tasks that are different in kind or degree from those with other media. Laboratory research has shown that these differences are related to differences in children's skills and knowledge. It has also shown that television medium characteristics, relatively independent of content, can be manipulated to produce changes in children's feelings and information-processing activities. Whether these effects also occur as a result of children's everyday television viewing is an unanswered question.

THE MEDIUM NOT THE MESSAGE

There can be no argument that television is a medium as well as messages. Without question it is a wondrous window on the world for children at home and at school, and its visions certainly affect children. But the medium itself also makes an impact on children. It takes much of their time each day, causing them to give up some activities, to do less of other activities, and to combine still other activities with television viewing. If they view a lot, children are likely to have less satisfactory peer relationships and to do less well in school than they otherwise might. However much they view, children can use the viewing as an opportunity to engage in or to avoid social interactions with family members. The medium also provokes parents to interact with children to regulate their viewing practices, and it provides children with conversation topics and play themes to use with both family members and peers. Finally, the medium—by necessity or by convention—involves certain perceptual stimuli, symbol systems, and aesthetics that make viewing an information-processing task with some different requirements and opportunities than those of other media. As a consequence, child viewers are likely to be learning certain skills and kinds of knowledge and not others. Thus, television is a multifaceted experience for children. It is the information-providing experience so many parents, social scientists, and social commentators have praised and decried, but it is also a time-consuming activity, a social or nonsocial event, and an information-processing task.

7

INFLUENCING TELEVISION'S ROLE IN CHILDREN'S LIVES

Television's impact on children can be influenced by having them engage in content-related activities surrounding viewing, by controlling their viewing practices, by teaching them to be literate viewers, and by changing television content and scheduling.

Children and television are often described as though they interact in a social and cultural vacuum. Television is examined as if it sprang up like Venus, pure and inviolate. Children are depicted as coming to television with certain given interests, needs, skills, and knowledge. Their interactions with the medium and its effects on them are treated as though they were immune to influence from children's parents, brothers and sisters, relatives, neighbors, religious leaders, teachers, club leaders, caregivers, and friends. The narrow vision arises from a need to explain simply how children interact with television, but the truth is more complex. Children and television function in social, cultural, and familial contexts that influence what messages children take away from television, how they use the medium, how literate they are as television viewers, what is broadcast on television, and when it is broadcast.

MODERATING EFFECTS OF TELEVISION MESSAGES

Much of the time and in many ways parents, teachers, and others can influence what messages children take away from television and what messages they use in their everyday lives. Opportunities for influence arise before, during, and after viewing when there are times for discussion, lecture, play, practice, testing, attention direction, explanation, and moral judgment. Some activities influence children's attention to, interpretation of, and learning of television messages. Others influence children's performance of messages they have already obtained from television content. Some activities help children to get more—and others help children to get less—out of television content (for research summaries see Chu & Schramm, 1979; Dorr, 1981; Leifer, 1976; and McLeod, Fitzpatrick, Glynn, & Fallis, 1982). We will describe these activities as though only parents and teachers engaged in them, but any child, adolescent, or adult with whom a child has contact can, and often does, do things before, during, and after viewing to moderate the effects of television messages on that child.

Activities Before Viewing

Before viewing, parents and teachers can engage in activities that affect children's interest in television messages, presumably thereby increasing or decreasing the amount of mental energy they invest in processing content (Salomon, 1983; see Chapter 6 for discussion) and hence increasing or decreasing learning. When television is used in schools, teachers can increase students' motivation to learn from programs by being enthusiastic themselves about the content, by showing how the content relates to children's interests, by explaining how the content can be used by children, and by scheduling a test on the content. Parents who want to encourage interest can do all the same things except that it is hard to threaten one's children with tests. When parents want to discourage interest, they can be unenthusiastic, describing how irrelevant and useless the television messages are and being careful not to make them attractive, forbidden fruit.

Children's learning of television messages is likely to increase when they are motivated viewers, but it can also be increased by judicious cognitive preparation before viewing. Giving children an overview or summary or schema for what they will see provides a cognitive map that makes it easier to process, understand, and remember messages as they occur during viewing. Explaining words, concepts, actions, settings, or implied content that are unfamiliar or hard to interpret is another technique for enhancing children's learning from programs, and it is much more effective before than after viewing. A third pre-viewing technique, describing the important messages or learning goals, increases children's learning of these messages while it simultaneously decreases learning other messages in the same television presentation.

Activities that start long before children view certain content can also be influential if they teach values that affect how children deal with television messages. For instance, past research has shown that youth who came to television with nonprejudiced racial attitudes recognized and recalled the liberal, antiprejudice messages in *All in the Family* (Vidmar & Rokeach, 1974) and that children whose families had taught them to value sugarless gum were likely to be swayed by a commercial for sugarless gum but not by one for sugared gum, even when their parents could not know what gum they chose (Esserman, 1981). To use this strategy successfully, parents and teachers must be very calculating. They must identify the value domains television messages address, teach the values they want children to have in each domain, and only then permit children to watch content that suggests different values.

Many pre-viewing activities seem at first blush to be for teachers, not parents, but that need not be the case. Without much planning, parents often communicate degrees of enthusiasm, relevance, and utility for the messages children are about to encounter. When my husband and I talk, in the presence of our five-year-old, about the great ideas in *Star Trek,* we are unintentionally—but no less effectively—influencing our son's motivation to attend to its messages. And parents certainly influence children's values in many areas. Moreover, parents sometimes foreshadow and summarize the messages in programs their children will see; for example, by explaining who George Washington was and the important role he played in founding our country before the family views a mini-series about his life. Pre-viewing activities may be more deliberately or more often chosen by teachers, but they are equally open to and effective for parents.

Activities During Viewing

During viewing parents and teachers can influence the effects of television's messages by directing children's attention toward and away from particular content. We know that children often look away from the television screen, sometimes stop listening to the audio track, and sometimes fail to look at the most important parts of the television picture. This is a normal part of the viewing activity that parents and teachers will sometimes want to influence so as to increase or decrease learning of the content being presented.

Parents and teachers can also enhance children's understanding and learning of content during viewing. At quiet points in the audio track, they can explain difficult content. Such explanations even work when they are broadcast on radio by an announcer whose comments are scripted to an advance copy of the program (Borton, Belasco, & Williams, 1975). Another way to increase learning during viewing is to provoke children to active participation in or rehearsal of content. For instance, learning the Japanese in the mini-series

Shogun would be enhanced if children repeated it as it was spoken or right afterward. Similarly, learning conceptual categories is promoted if children try to guess during the *Sesame Street* song "Three of these things belong together, three of these things are kinda the same. One of these things just doesn't belong here. Tell me, now, can you say its name?"

Finally, parents and teachers can influence children's post-viewing use of television messages by making evaluative comments about the messages during viewing. Parents who cheer the aggressive heroine and approve her tactics encourage their children to use aggression later, while parents who criticize her behavior discourage future aggression. For younger children, such evaluative commentary only seems to be effective in controlling behavior when the commentator is around, but for older children the comments guide subsequent behavior even when the commentator is absent (Grusec, 1973).

These proven strategies for influencing television content effects require teachers and parents to give time to viewing with children. Co-viewing is not always desired by or possible for parents, and teachers sometimes choose a television lesson precisely because they want to relax while it is on. But the benefits of co-viewing cannot be underplayed. Several studies have demonstrated that those children who view television programs such as *Sesame Street* with one or both parents learn more than do children who watch alone (Lesser, 1974; Salomon, 1977). Presumably, this is because co-viewing parents are engaging in the activities described here and perhaps, in addition, in pre-viewing or post-viewing activities based on what they know their children see on *Sesame Street*.

Activities After Viewing

After children have been exposed to television content, parents and teachers can influence its effects by the opportunities they do or do not provide for practice and feedback. They can offer or withhold relevant instructional materials, toys, or opportunities to practice. In terms of learning television content, the parent who buys *Picture Pages* for his or her child to complete after viewing this Bill Cosby program insert on Nickelodeon is making learning easier, while the parent who refuses to buy his or her child He-Man and She-Ra action figures to play with after viewing their cartoons is making it harder. The teacher who leaves time for a spirited discussion of the socioemotional messages in the instructional series *Inside/Out* is similarly choosing to influence students' learning.

Parents and teachers can also influence how much learning is displayed in everyday behavior by arranging children's environments so as to elicit or disinhibit such behavior or not. Suppose that American children have learned positive attitudes from watching *Big Blue Marble,* which features attractive vignettes about children living in many different countries. They cannot easily demonstrate these attitudes unless parents take them abroad or to an immigrant community. In the same way, but perhaps less obviously, parents and teachers daily organize children's lives so that some types of words and deeds are more likely than others. If they want to, they can establish environments that moderate how much children actually display what they have learned from television.

Evaluative reactions also influence how much television learning shows up in everyday behavior. Parents' and teachers' positive, neutral, or negative responses to a child's performance of some television content change the probability of future demonstrations of the same learning. Positive reactions encourage more, and negative reactions encourage less. Neutral reactions encourage actions that children believe are usually disapproved, discourage actions that children believe are usually approved, or have no effect. Evaluative commentaries—positive, neutral, or negative—about the television content itself (at a time when children are not performing it) will operate in a similar way to influence future demonstrations of that learned content.

While it is comforting to recognize that parents and teachers can influence children's performance of what they have learned from television content, that influence should not be exaggerated. Children who have learned behaviors that are fun or useful in everyday life are likely to display them even if discouraged by the adults in their environment. When younger, my older son had such fun executing karate chops and kicks learned from a Saturday cartoon series that he continued to perform them despite repeated disapprovals and punishments from me. Moreover, children find some television presentations much more compelling and convincing than are parents or teachers. Some commercials, for example, persuade children even if mothers argue against them (Prasad, Rao, & Sheikh, 1978). Recognizing these realities, some experts recommend being concerned, first and foremost, with what children watch, then with environmental opportunities to demonstrate learning, and only after that with evaluative comments and positive and negative reinforcements.

MODERATING USE OF THE TELEVISION MEDIUM

Children's use of the television medium can be described in terms of how much and when they watch, what they watch, and the setting in which they watch. When and how much children watch may be related to how well they do in school, in social interactions, and in sports and hobbies, as we saw in Chapter 6. What children watch is related to the kinds of information, attitudes, and behaviors they learn and perhaps perform, as we saw in Chapters 4 and 5. Where and with whom children watch may be related to what they learn and perhaps perform, as we saw in the first section of this chapter. There are, then, several important outcomes that follow from how children use the television medium.

What goes on in school is largely irrelevant here. Television is infrequently used there and, when it is used, it is used for desirable purposes. Moreover, children do not have options in school about how much or when they watch, what they watch, or where they watch; only teachers have these options. There are many books written to help teachers use television well in class, here we will focus on children's use of the medium at home (for summaries of relevant research see Dorr, 1981; and McLeod et al., 1982).

Amount and Time of Viewing

How much and when children watch television is organized to some extent by the requirements and opportunities of their daily lives and to some extent by rules established by their parents. When we described typical viewing times for children of different ages, it was clear that the realities of daily life put some upper limits on how much television children can view and confine to some extent the times when they can view. But these natural limits and boundaries still leave a lot of flexibility for children. How much do parents further limit and confine—or simply guide—children's viewing experiences?

Our best evidence is that most parents do not establish rules that seriously limit how much or when children can view. In one study, for example, 19% of first graders, 22% of sixth graders, and 9% of tenth graders reported that their parents currently set limits on their television viewing (Lyle & Hoffman, 1972a). In an earlier study from a different region of the country, somewhat less than half a sample of tenth and eleventh graders reported that there were rules for how late they could watch television (Greenberg & Dominick,

1969). More parents, in general, report rules than do their children, but not that many more. For example, 40% of the mothers of the first graders referred to above reported at least sometimes setting special hours when children could view and slightly more than 30% reported any restrictions on the total amount of time children could view (Lyle & Hoffman, 1972a). These studies and many others, then, suggest that parents set some rules about when and how much their children may view television, but the majority of parents do not set many rules nor many very restrictive rules.

There are certain types of rules parents are more and less likely to set about when and how much to view television. They are very likely to say that viewing may not occur until children are dressed for school, have done their chores, or have completed their homework. They are also very likely to take away television viewing privileges as punishment or to give special privileges as a reward. Also reasonably common are rules about how late at night children may view and whether viewing may occur during meals or homework or music practice. Least common are rules about the total amount of television children may view each day or every week. There are, then, more rules about the "when" of viewing than about the "how much" of viewing.

There are ways, other than rules, for influencing children's viewing patterns. One, to which we have already alluded, is the organization of children's activities. Parents who organize many formal activities for children outside the house (e.g., sports, church, clubs) and structure their activities at home (e.g., homework, chores, practice) are also decreasing children's opportunities to view television. A second influence is the models of television viewing behaviors parents themselves provide. Several studies have shown that parents who watch a lot of television can expect to have children who, on average, watch more television, but the relationship weakens as the children grow up. Since parents' ability to set and enforce rules about viewing will also decline as children grow into adolescence, it is worthwhile establishing good viewing patterns early in children's lives.

What Is Viewed

Influencing what content children view on television may be done through rules about what must, may, and may not be watched, interactions about what will be watched whenever the child co-views with another, and modeling of certain content choices. All three methods have been shown to influence what content children actually view. Research suggests that rules operate to constrain what some children view some of the time but that, like rules for when and how much to watch, content rules are not all that confining for most children. For interactions and modeling, there is only enough research to show that both processes can sometimes affect what children view.

No one will be surprised to learn that most rules declare some content to be off limits and that such rules are more common for younger than older children. Findings from three different studies illustrate the frequencies of rules about what to watch and the changes in rules as children mature: Among a sample of 3- and 4-year-olds about two-thirds believed someone else selected what they watched (Lyle & Hoffman, 1972b); among a sample of 6- to 12-year-olds less than half reported they could not generally watch what they wanted (Streicher & Bonney, 1974); and among a sample of tenth and eleventh graders about one-quarter reported some limits on the programs they could watch (Greenberg & Dominick, 1969). Again, more parents report having rules and having more rules than do their children, but even parents do not say they are very controlling of what their children watch on television.

Interactions between children and their siblings or parents about what will be watched together inevitably influence viewing choices. In one study in which mothers and children intended to co-view, mothers chose the program about 40% of the time, thereby determining what their children watched as well as what they did not watch (Bower, 1973). In another study, junior and senior high school students reported that they watched more news and violent programs when they co-viewed with their parents and more comedy when they co-viewed with younger siblings (Chaffee & Tims, 1976). How much older and younger siblings influence what children view is an open question now, but it seems unlikely that children's interactions with sibling co-viewers—or parent co-viewers, for that matter—are a major influence on what children watch.

Even when they are not co-viewing, parents' viewing choices can set an example for their children to follow. If parents are heavy viewers of public television or news and public affairs programming, their children are more likely to view more of each type of content than are other children. Again, though, modeling is a small influence among several small influences on what content children view. Mostly, what is viewed is up to the stations who choose what to broadcast when and up to the children who decide what to watch.

The Viewing Setting

Thinking back to the section "Moderating Effects of Television Messages," it is easy to see why the objects, activities, and people in a viewing setting could matter. Their presence or absence, what they are like, and what they do can influence how easily children will pay attention to programming, how much help they will get in understanding it, how they will value it, and how much they will participate actively in the content. The earlier descriptions of what home viewing is like suggest that there could be much variation across families and over time in these aspects of the viewing setting, but they have received little attention in our research.

A small proportion of children's viewing time is probably spent co-viewing with parents or other adults, a larger proportion of time—as much as half—is probably spent co-viewing with siblings, and most viewing settings are certainly full of objects and activities that are potentially distracting and not meant to produce active participation in or practice of content being presented on television. Social class and family size should influence how many televisions are in the household and how much solitary or undistracted viewing is possible, but there are no studies of what family characteristics determine the kinds of viewing settings they provide for their children. However it happens, influencing the settings in which children view television is another means of moderating children's use of the television medium. Influencing viewing settings, combined with influencing what children watch, when they watch, and how much they watch, are the main means by which parents can moderate their children's use of the medium.

DEVELOPING LITERATE VIEWERS

In the last decade a new approach, variously known as television literacy, critical viewing skills, or television receivership skills, has arisen for moderating television's role in children's lives. The idea is to teach children themselves to use the medium to its best advantage. There are three rationales for undertaking this task: (1) There is ample evidence children do not use the medium as well as they might; (2) the television industry, parents, teachers, and other adults are not likely to be as continuously solicitous of children as are children themselves; (3) television is a medium that requires literacy instruction just as the medium of print does. Several television literacy curricula have been developed and evaluated, giving good illustrations of usual goals, providing model curricula and hard data on what they can accomplish, and leaving some questions about the practical and political limitations of this approach (for reviews of television literacy efforts see Anderson, 1983; Corder-Bolz, 1982; and Dorr, 1985).

Television Literacy Goals

Only a few television literacy goals have been chosen as important enough to warrant curriculum development. Most focus on home viewing and on programming and advertising content on commercial stations. Based on the announced goals of existing curricula and those goals that can be easily inferred from the curricula, the following list is representative of the goals of today's television viewing skills curricula:

(1) Understand how television content is produced
(2) Understand the broadcasting system
(3) Understand types of stations, programming, and advertising
(4) Understand advertising goals and techniques
(5) Critically evaluate advertising content and be less influenced by it
(6) Recognize explicit and implicit values in content, especially those that are stereotyped and antisocial
(7) Critically evaluate the values in content and refrain from accepting those that are stereotyped or antisocial
(8) Recognize how much time is given to television viewing
(9) Give less time to television viewing
(10) Recognize the low quality of much of what is viewed
(11) Watch better quality programming
(12) Learn how to use viewing guides
(13) Use viewing guides to plan a viewing schedule

From an action perspective, goals 5, 7, 9, 11, and 13 are the crucial ones. If a curriculum is effective, not only will children understand the medium and recognize qualities of its content and of their use of it, they will also use television better in their everyday lives. Few can quarrel with the desirability of achieving these television literacy goals with children.

The accepted meanings of television literacy can be further elucidated by contrasting its goals to those for print and computer literacy. For television, there is no attempt to increase liking or decrease fear, whereas these are common goals for print and computer literacy curricula respectively. There is also no effort to teach use of the television set itself, while there is much emphasis on how to operate the input and output devices of a computer. For television, there is little emphasis on decoding of symbols and strings of symbols, on extracting meaning, and on understanding structure, whereas these elements are at the heart of print literacy efforts and certain symbols (e.g., the cursor) and structures (e.g., the menu) are part of virtually all computer literacy curricula. Finally, television literacy curricula rarely teach television production, whereas the other curricula teach writing and programming respectively. Thus there are some media literacy goals, such as decoding, interpretation, liking, and production, that are given short shrift in television literacy curricula, perhaps not altogether wisely.

There has been some criticism lately of many television literacy goals, mostly by the communications researcher James Anderson (1983). Although a developer of critical viewing skills curricula himself, he chides others for wrongly attempting to save children from television and to make them prematurely into adults. Arguing it is important that children live life on their own terms, create their own experiences, and enjoy themselves, Anderson explicitly rejects goals that emphasize changing taste, viewing less, being less affected, and employing adult paradigms for understanding and critiquing television. Moreover, he quite rightly reminds curriculum developers that they need to gear curricula more to the realities of everyday home viewing and of the educational establishment than to the demands of psychological theorizing and curriculum development. Anderson's criticisms are cogent, but they have not dissuaded him—nor should they dissuade others—from continuing to promote the value of properly conceived television literacy curricula.

Curriculum and Evaluation

Several different approaches have been used in television literacy curricula. A few curricula are for parents, assuming they will then teach their children, but most are for youth. We will focus on curricula for children from three to 18 years of age, some designed for use in school and others for use out of school. All involve imparting information about production and the television industry to children, most using the traditional methods of reading, lecture, and discussion and some including role playing, visiting production and broadcasting facilities, and viewing films and television programs. Some curricula tell about and demonstrate techniques for advertising and for conveying values. Others involve exercises, such as conducting a mini-content analysis of one's favorite programs, that should lead children themselves to recognize persuasion, bias, stereotypy, and antisocialness in television content. Some ask participants to keep viewing logs to help them recognize and evaluate their viewing choices. Like most curricula in other content areas, television literacy curricula are heavier on informing and lighter on processing, interpreting, evaluating, and behaving; and didactic methods are much more common than are experiential approaches to learning.

Most television literacy curricula shy away from complex delivery systems. There are a few interesting exceptions; for example, NBC produced short television literacy segments and broadcast them on Saturday morning and New York City's PBS station produced a television literacy curriculum. Most curricula, however, use books, with or without worksheets, and assume a teacher or leader will lecture and guide question and answer sessions and discussions. A few provide instructions for using props, toys, and other manipulables. A few use films or videotapes, and most require some television viewing at home. Virtually none uses video systems with which children produce their own programs. By and large, then, television literacy is not taught with television.

There have been only a few rigorous evaluations of television literacy curricula. In every one children learned the cognitive or informational content. Few have tested for, and even fewer shown, any impact on children's television-related behaviors—how much television they watch, what content they choose to watch, the meaning they construct for content, their critical evaluation of content, or use of content in everyday lives. A few studies, though, have shown effects beyond learning information: Children evaluated advertising claims more critically after some television literacy courses (Feshbach, Feshbach, & Cohen, 1982; Roberts, Christenson, Gibson, Mooser, & Goldberg, 1980); after one curriculum they reasoned differently about the reality and representativity of programs they watched at home (Dorr, Graves, & Phelps, 1980); and after another they identified less with aggressive protagonists and adopted fewer aggressive messages from programs they watched at home (Huesmann, Eron, Klein, Brice, & Fischer, 1983). To achieve these effects curricula must be more action and application oriented, going well beyond the simple presentation of information about television.

Practical and Political Limitations

In the never never land of easy solutions, television literacy curricula should achieve their best goals. After a semester or two of instruction, children should not only have more information about the medium but they should also watch it less, watch higher quality programs, respond reasonably to advertising, and reject stereotyped and antisocial messages. Unfortunately, there are real limitations to what we can expect television literacy curricula to achieve—even the very best curriculum delivered with consummate skill to eager students. Curricula cannot be sold as the panacea we have all been waiting for.

The potential societal benefits of television literacy curricula are further limited by substantial practical problems in delivering curricula to children. Because television literacy is not a top priority among parents or teachers, there is not enough consumer demand to support the free-market development and use of curricula. Curricula are most likely to be taught to those children whose parents and teachers can easily take care of high priority goals and have time left over. Other children could only be reached by broadcasts over commercial television stations at times most children are viewing, but for obvious reasons stations and networks are reluctant to delve too deeply into critical viewing skills. Given these practical limitations to the production and distribution of television literacy curricula, some have suggested that the federal government step in.

Political problems abound for government efforts at television literacy. Although federal and local funds have supported some curriculum development efforts, it is often hard to argue that today's limited resources should be diverted from more critical problem areas. Moreover, many believe networks and not taxpayers should finance curricula aimed at removing problems caused by the broadcasting industry itself. Finally, some view television literacy curricula as rather like blaming the victim. If children have problems with television, so the argument goes, it is because parents and teachers are not doing what they should to help children deal well with the medium and, most important of all, the television industry is shirking its responsibilities to avoid harm and to do good.

INFLUENCING TELEVISION CONTENT AND SCHEDULING

It is time now to turn to television. Our picture of the important participants in the child-television transaction would not be complete otherwise, but we will not dwell long on television production and scheduling, as they are best covered in books about broadcasting (e.g., Avery & Pepper, 1979; Barnouw, 1970; Cantor, 1980; Comstock, 1980; Gitlin, 1983; Turow, 1984; Wood & Wylie, 1977). We will only briefly examine how instructional, public, and commercial broadcasting systems determine what will be produced and when it will be broadcast, the influence of funding on content, and the role of regulation in influencing content and scheduling.

Organizational Influences

Television seen in the United States is almost always made by Americans for Americans. People who belong to our culture create programs and commercials that broadly reflect our culture and none other and are directed to our culture and none other. Anyone who has watched Mexican novelas, Japanese fairy tales, Swedish children's cartoons, French puppets, Middle Eastern shadow plays, or British comedians—and some of all this can be seen in America—will realize how different "our" television would be if it were mostly imported from other countries or produced by recent immigrants. In some countries much programming is imported from other countries, but in the United States it is homegrown, so that American culture very much influences the nature of the television each child encounters.

Instructional, public, and commerical broadcasting organizations are also responsive to consumer demands in their own market sectors. The instructional programs produced are those instructional broadcasters will buy or help finance after they canvass school personnel about their program needs. The Corporation for Public Broadcasting determines program purchases and new production largely by the programs' rank ordering by PBS stations who represent their own local audience's interests, with children just one part of their total audience. In commercial broadcasting, children's programming needs are rarely compelling, because children do not have much buying power, are not the largest segment of our society, and will watch much programming intended for other audiences (see Melody, 1973, for further discussion). There are, however, a few time periods (e.g., weekend mornings) when children are usually the most available audience, and some stations recognize some obligation to provide children's programming at other times. Finally, in large metropolitan areas one or more independent stations usually broadcast much programming aimed at children, because that is the best way to make money in these areas.

Since television production is a complex process, there are many opportunities for content to be reviewed and shaped to the interests of children. The three major networks, who are responsible for most programming children view at home, all periodically consult with advisers trained in child development, education, psychology, and/or communication. Each has a broadcast standards department that actively participates in the production process to assure adherence to such network standards as showing good taste, avoiding imitable undesirable actions, and refraining from gratuitous violence or sexuality. Networks also review all advertising for conformity to their standards, but they do not participate in its development. Most child advocates believe the networks, production companies, and advertising agencies could improve their production processes (e.g., Siegel, 1980), but none deny that they all now have some useful review and oversight mechanisms in operation.

Oversight by a broadcast standards department and a board of advisers is considered mostly unnecessary for public and instructional broadcasting, as their staffs are supposed to keep children's best interests in mind and to have had the training needed to make good children's programs. Many instructional programs and some PBS children's programs, however, employ content specialists, educators, communicationists, and/or child psychologists as advisers at certain points in a project. At times, they each also use formative research as an aid in developing attractive and effective children's programming.

Televised advertising to children is influenced by slightly different groups. Manufacturers employ advisers and research staff to guide development toward products and packaging attractive to children. Advertising agencies develop commercials and advertising campaigns that will be attractive, understandable, and persuasive for children, using outside advisers and internal and external formative research. Both manufacturers and advertising agencies internally review commercials and campaigns to be certain they conform to their own standards, those of the stations on which they intend to air the commercials, and those of self-regulatory agencies within the industry. Again, many child advocates have expressed dissatisfaction with these internal systems, while also recognizing that the industry sets some laudatory standards for itself, sets limits on how bad it can be, and operates internally to meet standards and stay within limits.

Funding Influences

Since all television content is expensive to produce, funding definitely influences what content is available for children. Over the years, Congress, federal agencies, private agencies, and foundations have determined that television could help achieve important goals in mathematics, science, substance abuse, nutrition, consumerism, computer literacy, preschool education, career awareness, teenage suicide, art appreciation, literature, child abuse and more. Earmarking funds for television production in such areas has always guaranteed that the content is soon available for broadcasting. There can even be a snowball effect when instructional, public, and commercial systems themselves fund programs imitating those externally funded programs that turned out to be popular. Relationships between funders and producers have always been tricky (see Rockman, 1980, for an illuminating discussion), but no one can deny the important influence of outside funding on what television content is available for children.

Regulatory Influences

Instructional, public, and commerical broadcasting systems all operate within a web of regulations and potential regulations that facilitate and constrain their content and scheduling, but the regulatory arena in which child advocates are most interested is that for commercial broadcasting. There are obvious reasons for this interest: Most television viewing time is given to programming and advertising broadcast on commercial stations; the most criticized content is broadcast on commerical stations; and the commercial broadcasting system is only moderately responsive to child advocates' criticisms and recommendations.

Many laws enacted by Congress and regulations established by the Federal Communications Commission (FCC) and the Federal Trade Commission (FTC) affect commercial broadcasting, but only four are especially relevant to children. One is that all commercial stations are licensed to broadcast in the public interest, convenience, and necessity. Most interpret this to mean that stations must broadcast content geared to their audience's interests, including the interests of children. A second law, the First Amendment guarantee of freedom of speech, generally restrains all efforts to establish standards for types of programs, broadcast schedules, and specific messages. The remaining two laws apply to advertising, one requiring that it not be deceptive and the other, that it be fair.

By and large, all advertisers, production companies, and broadcasters operate so as to conform to these laws and regulations, but child advocates have sought changes so as to decrease the amount of violence in programming, to promote more and better programming for children and better scheduling of it, and to protect children from advertising. Such political action began at least 30 years ago and continues today. It has resulted in few if any changes in laws and regulations and some changes, albeit often temporary, in the practices, standards, or voluntary regulations of those in the commercial broadcastig system.

Probably the earliest and most recurring political activity has been in response to concerns about violence in entertainment and informational programming (see Cater & Strickland, 1975; Rowland, 1983; and Rubinstein, 1980, for reviews). Congressional committees and presidential commissions have investigated what messages are presented about aggression and violence, what effects they have on viewers, and what can be done about the undesirable messages and effects. For every investigation, research information is summarized in written and oral testimony, and for a few, new research is commissioned as it was for the Surgeon General's study of television and social behavior and the subsequent hearings in the Senate Subcommittee on Communications. Issues are always hotly debated, and new laws or regulations rarely emerge. Most people agree, though, that focusing attention on the problem of televised violence has usually resulted in some desirable changes such as voluntary reductions in violent entertainment programs, advisories before violent programs, late airing of more objectionable content, and restricted news coverage of violent protests.

Efforts to provide more and better programming for children and to schedule it appropriately have been addressed to the FCC and recently to Congress. In 1970 Action for Children's Television (ACT), probably the oldest and most effective citizen action group in this area, petitioned the FCC that stations be required to broadcast a minimum number of hours of children's programming each week. Support for the request rested on research showing that children have special needs as an audience and that few beneficial age-appropriate programs were broadcast and on broadcasters' license obligations to their audience. Regulations were never adopted, but the FCC twice affirmed broadcasters' programming responsibilities to children. In the early 1980s virtually the same proposal, with the same rationale and outcome, appeared in a bill before Congress. More action is likely on this front.

Because there are clear First Amendment constraints to mandating more and better television content for children, other means to the same end have been sought. Technological change to increase the number of broadcast outlets and to provide pay services is always viewed as the most promising strategy, especially since the late 1970s when FCC staff found more children's programming in areas with many rather than few broadcasting outlets. Regulations have been proposed to provide more over-the-air commerical stations, to hasten the adoption of cable and pay television, and to promote home video systems, and a few have recently been adopted. The technologies that deliver television-like content have been changing rapidly in the last decade, but the content itself has not changed very much at all.

Televised advertising to children became a policy issue in the 1970s (see Adler, 1980; Choate, 1980; and Rossiter, 1980, for reviews). ACT's 1970 petition to the FCC included requests that children's programs have no sponsorship, no commercials, and no selling of products within programs or by program hosts. The FCC never adopted any regulations, but broadcasters voluntarily reduced advertising minutes per hour, banned host selling, and instituted separators between children's programs and advertisements. Advertisers established a self-regulatory group, the Children's Advertising Review Unit of the Council of Better Business Bureaus. Later in the 1970s the FTC proposed banning advertising to children too young to understand selling intent, banning advertising of sugared products to older children, and balancing any remaining advertising of sugared products with nutritional or health disclosures funded by advertisers. Again, no regulations were enacted, but the FTC's final report clearly argues that advertising to young children is inherently unfair (Federal Trade Commission, 1981).

Attempts to influence instructional or public television have centered almost exclusively on ensuring adequate, stable, and independent funding for such programming. Even these efforts have met with little success, as Congress apparently prefers to keep its power of the purse string. Whether or not one believes that changes are needed in the legal and regulatory structures of instructional, public, or commercial broadcasting, one must recognize that the present structures themselves influence television and hence influence the role of television in children's lives.

MAGIC WINDOWS AND BRAINS

Television and children each exist among people, organizations, systems, laws, and regulations that influence what they are like and how they interact with each other. Children develop interests, needs, abilities, experiences, knowledge, and television literacy that they bring with them to television. Television content and schedules are created by people in our culture, further structured by voluntary and involuntary regulations and laws, and then delivered to children. How much, when, and for what content children turn to television at home are to some extent influenced by family members and at school are to a large extent determined by teachers. What children understand and take away from their viewing can be very much influenced by the actions of other people before, during, and after children view. Altogether there are many points and many ways to influence the role that television plays in children's lives. Options abound for making television a magic window not an idiot box for children and for making children brains not boobs when it comes to using television.

The research reviewed in the latter chapters of this book demonstrates that television is important to children and that its role in their lives is well worth influencing. Chapter 4 showed how television content can and does affect socially significant information, attitudes, and behaviors of children. Chapter 5 described debates about the limitations of these television content effects and suggested what variables determine effect size and generality. Chapter 6 extended our notion of effects to include enhancement of the attitudes and information-processing skills called for by television and illustrated how much of children's everyday lives is given over to or conducted in the presence of television. These three chapters, then, clearly demonstrate that television, the magic window and the idiot box, now plays a role in children's lives, and they provide social activists with several reasons to urge greater care with what is broadcast and viewed on instructional, public, and commerical television. They also suggest several means for producing more and less impactful content for children.

Research on how children construct meaning for television content (Chapters 2 and 3) provides several ideas about how to produce more and less understandable content for children. Chapter 2 presented the many information-processing, interpretive, and evaluative tasks often required to make sense of television content, and Chapter 3 described how different types of children, especially children of different ages, carried out these tasks. Together the chapters clearly demonstrate that television content produced without any special concern for children can easily be too difficult for them to understand as the producer intended. Programming in the best interests of children, programming that brings to life television's promise as a magic window, requires producing especially *for children's* information-processing, interpretive, and evaluative methods and skills.

Information about the children-television transaction and the larger familial, social, and cultural context in which it occurs provides intellectual stimulation for scholars and practical ammunition for activists. In the last three decades, social scientists have identified and put together several pieces of the puzzle of how children use television and how they are used by it. Many pieces are still missing, and others need some reshaping. The challenge to scholars remains.

At the same time, scholars have already produced knowledge useful for practice and policy. Research information can help produce programs and commercials that will be understood, will lead to intended content and skill outcomes, and will have salutary effects on children; it can help shape voluntary and involuntary regulations of programs and commercial advertising to children; and it can help parents and teachers know when and how to monitor, guide, and/or control their children's experiences with television. It can help make television a wondrous magic window for children and help those responsible for children to use television so that it becomes a magic window. Research can also help with the development of television literacy curricula and with the advice given to parents and teachers so that they can all teach children to become brains when it comes to television, to take advantage of the good the medium offers and to avoid the bad. Hackneyed though the sentiment may be, children are our most important resource. They are also, then, an important audience for that important medium television. With the knowledge we have today we can do much to make the transaction between children and television a good one.

REFERENCES

Adler, R. P. (1980). Children's television advertising: History of the issue. In E. L. Palmer & A. Dorr (Eds.), *Children and the faces of television—teaching, violence, selling.* New York: Academic Press.

Adler, R. P., Lesser, G. S., Meringoff, L., Robertson, T. S., Rossiter, J. R., & Ward, S. (1980). *The effects of television advertising on children.* Lexington, MA: Lexington Books.

Alper, S. W., & Leidy, T. R. (1970). The impact of information transmission through television. *Public Opinion Quarterly, 33,* 556-562.

Almstead, F. E., & Graf, R. W. (1960). Talkback: The missing ingredient. *Audio-Visual Instruction, 5,* 110-112.

Alwitt, L. F., Anderson, D. R., Lorch, E. P., & Levin, S. R. (1980). Preschool children's visual attention to attributes of television. *Human Communication Research, 7,* 52-67.

Anderson, D. R., Levin, S. R., & Lorch, E. P. (1977). The effects of TV program pacing on the behavior of preschool children. *AV Communication Review, 25* (2), 159-166.

Anderson, D. R., & Lorch, E. P. (1983). Looking at television: Action or reaction? In J. Bryant & D. R. Anderson (Eds.), *Children's understanding of television: Research on attention and comprehension.* New York: Academic Press.

Anderson, J. A. (1981). Research on children and television: A critique. *Journal of Broadcasting, 25* (4), 395-400.

Anderson, J. A. (1983). Television literacy and the critical viewer. In J. Bryant & D. R. Anderson (Eds.), *Children's understanding of television: Research on attention and comprehension.* New York: Academic Press.

Atkin, C. K. (1982). Television advertising and socialization to consumer roles. In D. Pearl, L. Bouthilet, & J. Lazar (Eds.), *Television and behavior: Ten years of scientific progress and implications for the eighties* (Vol. 2). (DHHS Publication No. ADM 82-1196). Washington, DC: U. S. Government Printing Office.

Avery, R. K., & Pepper, R. (1979). *The politics of interconnection: A history of public television at the national level.* Washington, DC: National Association of Educational Broadcasters.

Ballard-Campbell, M. (1983). *Children's understanding of television advertising: Behavioral assessment of three developmental skills.* Unpublished doctoral dissertation, University of California, Los Angeles.

Bandura, A. (1973). *Aggression: A social learning analysis.* Englewood Cliffs, NJ: Prentice-Hall.

Bandura, A. (1977). *Social learning.* Englewood Cliffs, NJ: Prentice-Hall.

Bandura, A. (1978). Social learning theory of aggression. *Journal of Communication, 28* (3), 12-29.

Bandura, A., Ross, D., & Ross, S. A. (1961). Transmission of aggression through imitation of aggressive models. *Journal of Abnormal and Social Psychology, 63,* 575-582.

Bandura, A., Ross, D., & Ross, S. A. (1963a). Imitation of film-mediated aggressive models. *Journal of Abnormal and Social Psychology, 66,* 3-11.

Bandura, A., Ross, D., & Ross, S. A. (1963b). Vicarious reinforcement and imitative learning. *Journal of Abnormal and Social Psychology, 66,* 601-607.

Barnouw, E. (1970). *The image empire: A history of broadcasting in the United States from 1953.* New York: Oxford University Press.

Belson, W. (1978). *Television violence and the adolescent boy.* London: Saxon House.

Berger, P. L., & Luckmann, T. (1966). *The social construction of reality.* New York: Doubleday.

Berkowitz, L. (1962). *Aggression: A social psychological analysis.* New York: McGraw-Hill.

Berkowitz, L. (1973). Words and symbols as stimuli to aggressive responses. In J. F. Knutson (Ed.), *Control of aggression: Implications from basic research.* Chicago: Aldine-Atherton.

Blumler, J. G., & Katz, E. (Eds.). (1974). *The uses of mass communications.* Beverly Hills, CA: Sage.

Borton, T., Belasco, L., & Williams, A. R. (1975). Dual audio television goes public. *Journal of Communication, 25* (3), 61-68.

Bower, R. T. (1973). *Television and the public.* New York: Holt, Rinehart and Winston.

Brown, J. R. (1976). Children's uses of television. In R. Brown (Ed.), *Children and television.* Beverly Hills, CA: Sage.

Burdach, K. J. (1983). Methodological aspects of formative research. In M. Meyer (Ed.), *Children and the formal features of television: Approaches and findings of experimental and formative research.* Munich and New York: K. G. Saur.

Cantor, M. G. (1980). *Prime-time television: Content and control.* Beverly Hills, CA: Sage.

Cater, D., & Strickland, S. (1975). *TV violence and the child: The evolution and fate of the Surgeon General's Report.* New York: Russell Sage Foundation.

Chaffee, S. H., & Tims, A. R. (1976). Interpersonal factors in adolescent television use. *Journal of Social Issues, 32,* 98-115.

Choate, R. B. (1980). The politics of change. In E. L. Palmer & A. Dorr (Eds.), *Children and the faces of television—teaching, violence, selling.* New York: Academic Press.

Chu, G. C., & Schramm, W. (1979). *Learning from television: What the research says.* Washington, DC: National Association of Educational Broadcasters.

Clancy-Hepburn, K., Hickey, A., & Neville, G. (1974). Children's behavior responses to TV food advertisements. *Journal of Nutrition Education, 6,* 93-96.

Clark, R. E. (1983). Reconsidering research on learning from media. *Review of Educational Research, 53,* 445-459.

Collins, W. A. (1982). Cognitive processing in television viewing. In D. Pearl, L. Bouthilet, & J. Lazar (Eds.), *Television and behavior: Ten years of scientific progress and implications for the eighties* (Vol. 2). (DHHS Publication No. ADM82-1196). Washington, DC: U.S. Government Printing Office.

Collins, W. A. (1983). Interpretation and inference in children's television viewing. In J. Bryant & D. R. Anderson (Eds.), *Children's understanding of television: Research on attention and comprehension.* New York: Academic Press.

Collins, W. A., Berndt, T. J., & Hess, V. L. (1974). Observational learning of motives and consequences for television aggression: A developmental study. *Child Development, 45,* 799-802.

Comstock, G. (1980). *Television in America.* Beverly Hills, CA: Sage.

Comstock, G. (1983). Media influences on aggression. In A. Goldstein (Ed.), *Prevention and control of aggression.* New York: Pergamon Press.

Comstock, G. (in press). Television and film violence. In S. J. Apter & A. P. Goldstein (Eds.), *Youth violence: Programs and prospects.* New York: Pergamon Press.

Comstock, G., Chaffee, S., Katzman, N., McCombs, M., & Roberts, D. (1978). *Television and human behavior.* New York: Columbia University Press.

Cook, T. D., Kendzierski, D. A., & Thomas, S. V. (1983). The implicit assumptions of television research: An analysis of the 1982 NIMH Report on television and behavior. *Public Opinion Quarterly, 47,* 161-201.

Corder-Bolz, C. R. (1982). Television literacy and critical television viewing skills. In D. Pearl, L. Bouthilet, & J. Lazar (Eds.), *Television and behavior: Ten years of scientific progress and implications for the eighties* (Vol. 2). (DHHS Publication No. ADM82-1196). Washington, DC: U. S. Government Printing Office.

Cramond, J. (1976) The introduction of television and its effects upon children's daily lives. In R. Brown (Ed.), *Children and television.* Beverly Hills, CA: Sage.

Crane, V. (1980). Content development for children's television programs. In E. L. Palmer & A. Dorr (Eds.), *Children and the faces of television—teaching, violence, selling.* New York: Academic Press.

Dorr, A. (1980). When I was child, I thought as a child. In S. B. Withey & R. P. Abeles (Eds.), *Television and social behavior: Beyond violence and children.* Hillsdale, NJ: Lawrence Erlbaum.

Dorr, A. (1981). Interpersonal factors mediating viewing and effects. In G. V. Coelho (Ed.), *Television as a teacher: A research monograph* (#1981-341-166/6376). Washington, DC: U. S. Government Printing Office.

Dorr, A. (1983). No shortcuts to judging reality. In J. Bryant & D. R. Anderson (Eds.), *Children's understanding of television: Research on attention and comprehension.* New York: Academic Press.

Dorr, A. (1985). Television studies. In T. Husen & N. Postlethwaithe (Eds.), *International encyclopedia of education: Research and studies.* Oxford, England: Pergamon Press.

Dorr, A., Doubleday, C., & Kovaric, P. (1983). Emotions depicted on and stimulated by television programs. In M. Meyer (Ed.), *Children and the formal features of television: Approaches and findings of experimental and formative research.* Munich and New York: K. G. Saur.

Dorr, A., Graves, S. B., & Phelps, E. (1980). Television literacy for young children. *Journal of Communication, 30* (3), 71-83.

Dorr, A., & Kovaric, P. (1980). Some of the people some of the time—but which people? Televised violence and its effects. In E. L. Palmer & A. Dorr (Eds.), *Children and the faces of television—teaching, violence, selling.* New York: Academic Press.

Elliott, P. (1972). *The making of a television series: A case study in the sociology of culture.* Beverly Hills, CA: Sage.

Esserman, J. F. (1981). A study of children's defenses against television commercial appeals. In J. F. Esserman (Ed.), *Television advertising and children: Issues, research and findings.* New York: Child Research Service.

Federal Trade Commission. (1981, March). *Final staff report and recommendation.* Washington, DC: U.S. Government Printing Office.

v. Feilitzen, C. (1976). The functions served by the media: Report on a Swedish study. In R. Brown (Ed.), *Children and television.* Beverly Hills, CA: Sage.

Fernie, D. E. (1981). Ordinary and extraordinary people: Children's understanding of television and real life models. In H. Kelly & H. Gardner (Eds.), *Viewing children through television.* San Francisco: Jossey-Bass.

Feshbach, S. (1955). The drive reducing function of fantasy behavior. *Journal of Abnormal and Social Psychology, 50,* 3-11.

Feshbach, S. (1961). The stimulating versus cathartic effects of vicarious aggressive activity. *Journal of Abnormal and Social Psychology, 63,* 381-385.

Feshbach, S., Feshbach, N. D., & Cohen, S. E. (1982). Enhancing children's discrimination in response to television advertising: The effects of psychoeducational training in two elementary school-age groups. *Developmental Review, 2,* 385-403.

Feshbach, S., & Singer, R. D. (1971). *Television and aggression.* San Francisco: Jossey-Bass.

Flagg, B. N., Housen, A., & Lesser, S. (1978, June). *Pre-reading and pre-science on "Sesame Street."* Unpublished manuscript, Harvard University.

Freedman, J. L. (1984). Effects of television violence on aggressiveness. *Psychological Bulletin, 96,* 227-246.

Friedrich, L. K., & Stein, A. H. (1973). Aggressive and prosocial television programs and the naturalistic behavior of preschool children. *Monographs of the Society for Research in Child Development, 38* (4, Serial No. 151).

Frueh, T., & McGhee, P. E. (1975). Traditional sex role development and amount of time spent watching television. *Developmental Psychology, 11,* 109.

Gerbner, G., & Gross, L. (1980). The violent face of television and its lessons. In E. L. Palmer & A. Dorr (Eds.), *Children and the faces of television—teaching, violence, selling.* New York: Academic Press.

Gerbner, G., Gross, L., Morgan, M., & Signorielli, N. (1980). The "mainstreaming" of America: Violence Profile No. 11. *Journal of Communication, 30* (3), 10-29.

Gitlin, T. (1983). *Inside prime time.* New York: Pantheon.

Goffman, E. (1974). *Frame analysis: An essay on the organization of experience.* Cambridge, MA: Harvard University Press.

Goodman, N. (1968). *The languages of art.* Indianapolis: Hackett.

Gore Vidal: His life is an opened book. (1984, July 15). *Los Angeles Times,* pp. 1, 10, 11.

Gorn, G. J., Goldberg, M. E., & Kanungo, R. N. (1976). The role of educational television in changing intergroup attitudes of children. *Child Development, 47,* 227-280.

Greenberg, B. S., & Dominick, J. R. (1969). Racial and social class differences in teenagers' use of television. *Journal of Broadcasting, 13,* 331-344.

Greenfield, P. M. (1984). *Mind and media: The effects of television, video games, and computers.* Cambridge, MA: Harvard University Press.

Grusec, J. E. (1973). Effects of co-observer evaluations on imitation: A developmental study. *Developmental Psychology, 8,* 141.

Hawkins, R. P. (1977). The dimensional structure of children's perceptions of television reality. *Communication Research, 4,* 299-320.

Hawkins, R. P., Pingree, S., & Roberts, D. F. (1975). Watergate and political socialization: The inescapable event. *American Politics Quarterly, 3,* 406-422.

Hayakawa, S. I. (1968, September). *Mass media and family communications.* Paper presented at the annual meeting of the American Psychological Association, San Francisco.

Himmelweit, H. T., Oppenheim, A. N., & Vince, P. (1958). *Television and the child.* London: Oxford University Press.

Holaday, P. W., & Stoddard, G. D. (1933). *Getting ideas from the movies.* New York: Macmillan.

Hornik, R., Gonzalez, M., & Gould, J. (1980, May). *Susceptibility to media effects.* Paper presented at the annual meeting of the International Communication Association, Acapulco, Mexico.

Huesmann, L. R., Eron, L. D., Klein, R., Brice, P., & Fischer, P. (1983). Mitigating the imitation of aggressive behaviors by changing children's attitudes about media violence. *Journal of Personality and Social Psychology, 44,* 899-910.

Hussey, D. (1963). *Verdi.* London: J. M. Dent.

Huston, A. C., Greer, D., Wright, J. C., Welch, R., & Ross, R. (1984). Children's comprehension of televised formal features with masculine and feminine connotations. *Developmental Psychology, 20,* 707-716.

Huston, A. C., & Wright, J. C. (1983). Children's processing of television: The informative functions of formal features. In J. Bryant & D. R. Anderson (Eds.), *Children's understanding of television: Research on attention and comprehension.* New York: Academic Press.

Kenny, D. A. (1972). Threats to the internal validity of cross-lagged panel inference, as related to "Television violence and child aggression: A followup study." In G. A. Comstock & E. A. Rubinstein (Eds.), *Television and social behavior: Vol. 3. Television and adolescent aggressiveness.* Washington, DC: U. S. Government Printing Office.

Kenny, D. A. (1984). The NBC study and television violence: A review. *Journal of Communication, 34* (1), 176-188.

Kline, F. G., Miller, P. V., & Morrison, A. J. (1974). Adolescents and family planning information: An exploration of audience needs and media effects. In J. G. Blumler & E. Katz (Eds.), *The uses of mass communications.* Beverly Hills, CA: Sage.

Kosinski, J. (1970). *Being there.* New York: Harcourt Brace Jovanovich.

Krull, R. (1983). Children learning to watch television. In J. Bryant & D. R. Anderson (Eds.), *Children's understanding of television: Research on attention and comprehension.* New York: Academic Press.

Lefkowitz, M. M., Eron, L. D., Walder, L. O., & Huesmann, L. R. (1972). Television violence and child aggression: A followup study. In G. A. Comstock & E. A. Rubinstein (Eds.), *Television and social behavior: Vol. 3. Television and adolescent aggressiveness.* Washington, DC: U.S. Government Printing Office.

Leifer, A. D. (1976). Teaching with television and film. In N. L. Gage (Ed.), *Psychology of teaching methods.* Chicago: University of Chicago Press.

Leifer, A. D., & Roberts, D. F. (1972). Children's responses to television violence. In J. P. Murray, E. A. Rubinstein, & G. A. Comstock (Eds.), *Television and social behavior: Vol. 2. Television and social learning.* Washington, DC: U.S. Government Printing Office.

Lesser, G. S. (1974). *Children and television: Lessons from Sesame Street.* New York: Random House.

Liebert, D., Sprafkin, J., Liebert, R., & Rubinstein, E. (1977). Effects of television commercial disclaimers on the product expectations of children. *Journal of Communication, 27* (1), 118-124.

Lull, J. (1980). The social uses of television. *Human Communication Research, 6,* 197-209.

Lyle, J., & Hoffman, H. R. (1972a). Children's use of television and other media. In E. A. Rubinstein, G. A. Comstock, & J. P. Murray (Eds.), *Television and social behavior: Vol. 4. Television in day-to-day life: Patterns of use.* Washington, DC: U.S. Government Printing Office.

Lyle, J., & Hoffman, H. R. (1972b). Explorations in patterns of television viewing by preschool-age children. In E. A. Rubinstein, G. A. Comstock, & J. P. Murray (Eds.), *Television and social behavior: Vol. 4. Television in day-to-day life: Patterns of use.* Washington, DC: U.S. Government Printing Office.

Maccoby, E. E., & Wilson, W. C. (1957). Identification and observational learning from films. *Journal of Abnormal and Social Psychology, 55,* 76-87.

Mander, J. (1978). *Four arguments for the elimination of television.* New York: William Morrow.

Mankiewicz, F., & Swerdlow, J. (1978). *Remote control: Television and the manipulation of American life.* New York: Times Books.

McLeod, J. M., Fitzpatrick, M. A., Glynn, C. J., & Fallis, S. F. (1982). Television and social relations: Family influences and consequences for interpersonal behavior. In D. Pearl, L. Bouthilet, & J. Lazar (Eds.), *Television and behavior: Ten years of scientific progress and implications for the eighties* (vol. 2). (DHHS Publication No. ADM82-1196). Washington, DC: U.S. Government Printing Office.

McLuhan, M. (1964). *Understanding media: The extensions of man.* New York: McGraw-Hill.

Melody, W. (1973). *Children's television.* New Haven, CT: Yale University Press.

Meringoff, L. K. (1980). Influence of the medium on children's story apprehension. *Journal of Educational Psychology, 72* (2), 240-249.

Meyer, M. (Ed.). (1983). *Children and the formal features of television: Approaches and findings of experimental and formative research.* Munich and New York: K. G. Saur.

Mielke, K. W. (1983). The educational use of production variables and formative research in programming. In M. Meyer (Ed.), *Children and the formal features of television: Approaches and findings of experimental and formative research.* Munich and New York: K. G. Saur.

Milavsky, J. R., Kessler, R. C., Stipp, H. H., & Rubens, W. S. (1982). *Television and aggression: A panel study.* New York: Academic Press.

Milgram, S., & Shotland, R. L. (1973). *Television and antisocial behavior: Field experiments.* New York: Academic Press.

Murray, J. P. (1980). *Television and youth.* Boys Town, NE: Boys Town Center for the Study of Youth Development.

National Education Association. (1980). *Nationwide teacher opinion poll 1980.* Washington, DC: Author.

Neale, J. M. (1972). Comment on "Television violence and child aggression: A followup study." In G. A. Comstock & E. A. Rubinstein (Eds.), *Television and social behavior: Vol. 3. Television and adolescent aggressiveness.* Washington, DC: U.S. Government Printing Office.

Nelson, B., & Napior, D. (1976). *Formative evaluation of the Rebop II pilot.* Cambridge, MA: Abt Associates.

Newcomb, A. F., & Collins, W. A. (1979). Children's comprehension of family role portrayals in televised dramas: Effects of socioeconomic status, ethnicity, and age. *Developmental Psychology, 15,* 417-423.

Noble, G. (1975). *Children in front of the small screen.* Beverly Hills, CA: Sage.

Olson, D. (Ed.). (1974). *Media and symbols: The forms of expression, communication, and education.* Chicago: University of Chicago Press.

Olson, D., & Bruner, J. (1974). Learning through experience and learning through media. In D. Olson (Ed.), *Media and symbols: The forms of expression, communication, and education.* Chicago: University of Chicago Press.

Palmer, E. L. (1983). Formative research in the production of television for children. In M. Meyer (Ed.), *Children and the formal features of television: Approaches and findings of experimental and formative research.* Munich and New York: K. G. Saur.

Palmer, E. L., & McDowell, C. N. (1979). The program commercial separators in children's television programming. *Journal of Communication, 29* (3), 197-201.

Parke, R. D., Berkowitz, L., Leyens, J. P., West, S. G., & Sebastian, R. J. (1977). Some effects of violent and nonviolent movies on the behavior of juvenile delinquents. In L. Berkowitz (Ed.), *Advances in experimental social psychology* (Vol. 10). New York: Academic Press.

Peterson, P. E., Jeffrey, D. B., Bridgewater, C. A., & Dawson, B. (1984). How pronutrition television programming affects children's dietary habits. *Developmental Psychology, 20,* 55-63.

Pingree, S. (1978). The effects of nonsexist television commercials and perceptions of reality on children's attitudes about women. *Psychology of Women Quarterly, 2,* 262-277.

Plato. (1952). *The Republic.* In R. M. Hutchins (Ed.), *Great books of the western world.* Chicago: Encyclopedia Britannica.

Postman, N. (1982). *The disappearance of childhood.* New York: Delacorte.

Prasad, V. K., Rao, T. R., & Sheikh, A. A. (1978). Mother vs. commercial. *Journal of Communication, 28* (1), 91-96.

Reeves, B., & Wartella, E. (1985). Historical trends in research on children and the media: 1900-1960. *Journal of Communication,* 35 (2), 118-133.

Rice, M. L., Huston, A. C., & Wright, J. C. (1982). The forms of television: Effects on children's attention, comprehension, and social behavior. In D. Pearl, L. Bouthilet, & J. Lazar (Eds.), *Television and behavior: Ten years of scientific progress and implications for the eighties* (Vol. 2). (DHHS Publication No. ADM82-1196). Washington, DC: U.S. Government Printing Office.

Roberts, D. F., Christenson, P., Gibson, W. A., Mooser, L., & Goldberg, M. E. (1980). Developing discriminating consumers. *Journal of Communication, 30* (3), 94-105.

Rockman, S. (1980). Realities of change. In E. L. Palmer & A. Dorr (Eds.), *Children and the faces of television—teaching, violence, selling.* New York: Academic Press.

Rockman, S. (1983). Formative research and evaluation of instructional television programs. In M. Meyer (Ed.), *Children and the formal features of television: Approaches and findings of experimental and formative research.* Munich and New York: K. G. Saur.

Rossiter, J. R. (1980). Children and television advertising: Policy issues, perspectives, and the status of research. In E. L. Palmer & A. Dorr (Eds.), *Children and the faces of television—teaching, violence, selling.* New York: Academic Press.

Rowland, W. D., Jr. (1983). *The politics of TV violence: Policy uses of communication research.* Beverly Hills, CA: Sage.

Rubin, A. M. (1979). Television use by children and adolescents. *Human Communication Research, 5,* 109-120.

Rubin, A. M., & Rubin, R. B. (1982). Contextual age and television use. *Human Communication Research, 8,* 228-244.

Rubinstein, E. A. (1980). Television violence: A historical perspective. In E. L. Palmer & A. Dorr (Eds.), *Children and the faces of television—teaching, violence, selling.* New York: Academic Press.

Rubinstein, E. A., & Sprafkin, J. N. (1982). Television and persons in institutions. In D. Pearl, L. Bouthilet, & J. Lazar (Eds.), *Television and behavior: Ten years of scientific progress and implications for the eighties* (Vol. 2). (DHHS Publication No. ADM 82-1196). Washington, DC: U.S. Government Printing Office.

Rydin, I. (1983). How children understand television and learn from it: A Swedish perspective. In M. Meyer (Ed.), *Children and the formal features of television: Approaches and findings of experimental and formative research.* Munich and New York: K. G. Saur.

Salomon, G. (1977). Effects of encouraging Israeli mothers to co-observe *Sesame Street* with their five-year-olds. *Child Development, 48,* 1146-1151.

Salomon, G. (1979). *Interaction of media, cognition, and learning.* San Francisco: Jossey-Bass.

Salomon, G. (1983). Television watching and mental effort: A social psychological view. In J. Bryant & D. R. Anderson (Eds.), *Children's understanding of television: Research on attention and comprehension.* New York: Academic Press.

Salomon, G. (1984). Television is "easy" and print is "tough": The differential investment of mental effort in learning as a function of perceptions and attributions. *Journal of Educational Psychology, 76,* 647-658.

Schramm, W. (1972). What the research says. In W. Schramm (Ed.), *Quality in instructional television.* Honolulu: University Press of Hawaii.

Schramm, W. (1977). *Big media, little media: Tools and technologies for instruction.* Beverly Hills, CA: Sage.

Schramm, W., Lyle, J., & Parker, E. B. (1961). *Television in the lives of our children.* Stanford, CA: Stanford University Press.

Siegel, A. E. (1980). Research findings and social policy. In E. L. Palmer & A. Dorr (Eds.), *Children and the faces of television—teaching, violence, selling.* New York: Academic Press.

Singer, J. L., & Singer, D. G. (1983). Psychologists look at television: Cognitive, developmental, personality, and social policy implications. *American Psychologist, 38,* 826-834.

Sprafkin, J. N., Liebert, R. M., & Poulos, R. W. (1975). Effects of a pro-social televised example on children's helping. *Journal of Experimental Child Psychology, 20* (1), 119-126.

Steuer, F. B., Applefield, J. M., & Smith, R. (1971). Televised aggression and the interpersonal aggression of preschool children. *Journal of Experimental Child Psychology, 11,* 442-447.

Streicher, L. H., & Bonney, N. L. (1974). Children talk about television. *Journal of Communication, 24* (3), 54-61.

Tannenbaum, P. H., & Zillmann, D. (1975). Emotional arousal in the facilitation of aggression through communication. In L. Berkowitz (Ed.), *Advances in experimental social psychology* (Vol. 8). New York: Academic Press.

Turow, J. (1984). *Media industries: The production of news and entertainment.* New York: Longman.

Vidmar, N., & Rokeach, M. (1974). Archie Bunker's bigotry: A study in selective perception and exposure. *Journal of Communication, 24* (1), 36-47.

Ward, S., Wackman, D., & Wartella, E. (1977). *Consumer socialization: An information processing approach to consumer learning.* Beverly Hills, CA: Sage.

Wartella, E. (1980). Individual differences in children's responses to television advertising. In E. L. Palmer & A. Dorr (Eds.), *Children and the faces of television—teaching, violence, selling.* New York: Academic Press.

Watt, J. H., Jr., & Welch, A. J. (1983). Effects of static and dynamic complexity on children's attention and recall of televised instruction. In J. Bryant & D. R. Anderson (Eds.), *Children's understanding of television: Research on attention and comprehension.* New York: Academic Press.

Wood, D., & Wylie, D. (1977). *Educational telecommunications.* Belmont, CA: Wadsworth.

Worth, S., & Adair, J. (1972). *Through Navajo eyes: An exploration in anthropology and film communication.* Bloomington: Indiana University Press.

Wright, J. C., Huston, A. C., Ross, R. P., Calvert, S. L., Rolandelli, D., Weeks, L. A., Raeissi, P., & Potts, R. (1984). Pace and continuity of television programs: Effects on children's attention and comprehension. *Developmental Psychology, 20,* 653-666.

Yankelovich, S., & White, M. C. (1977). *The General Mills American family report, 1976-77: Raising children in a changing society.* Minneapolis: General Mills.

INDEX

AIMÉE DC rsity of
California, Ph.D. in
developm he held
academic rsity, in
education chool of
Communic he was a
contributo sion and
Social Beh report.
She is the *vision—*
Teaching, author
of more th ildren's
transactio viser to
numerous assachu-
setts Educa rkshop,
KCET, and ion and
self-regula and the
Childen's Business
Bureaus, as a consultant to the Federal Communications Commission, and as an expert witness before the Federal Trade Commission. She enjoys developing new knowledge about children's interactions with television and applying research knowledge to production, broadcasting, and regulatory decision making.